About this book

Symbols are used to denote the following categories:

- map reference to maps on cover
- address or location
- telephone number
- opening times
- admission charge
- restaurant or café on premises or nearby
- nearest underground train station
- nearest bus/tram route
- nearest overground train station
- nearest ferry stop
- nearest airport
- other practical information
- tourist information office
- ➤ indicates the page where you will find a fuller description

This book is divided into five sections.

The essence of Mexico pages 6–19
Introduction; Features; Food and drink; Short break including the 10 Essentials

Planning pages 20–33
Before you go; Getting there; Getting around; Being there

Best places to see pages 34–55
The unmissable highlights of any visit to Mexico

Best things to do pages 56–75
Good places to have lunch; top activities; best beaches, places to take the children and more

Exploring pages 76–185
The best places to visit in Mexico, organized by area

to denotes AAA rating

Maps

All map references are to the maps on the covers. For example, Palenque has the reference 21K – indicating the grid square in which it is to be found

Prices

An indication of the cost of restaurants at attractions is given by $ signs: $$$ denotes higher prices, $$ denotes average prices, $ denotes lower prices

Hotel prices

Price are per room per night: $ budget (under $250 pesos); $$ moderate ($250–$600 pesos); $$$ expensive to luxury (over $600 pesos)

Restaurant prices

Price for a three-course meal per person without drinks: $ budget (under $100 pesos); $$ moderate ($100–$150 pesos); $$$ expensive (over $150 pesos)

Contents

The essence of...

Few nations can rival Mexico's turbulent history, and few can claim such a cultural diversity. From the enigmatic giant heads of the Olmecs and the baroque outpourings of the Spaniards, to the stark clean lines of contemporary architecture and time-honored skills of the craftspeople, Mexico proudly displays a richly creative pulse. Reflecting this are the contrasts of the land itself – tropical rain forests in Chiapas, desert in Baja California, volcanoes and lakes in the center and *cenotes* (sinkholes) in the Yucatán. It is a country that excites, stimulates and awes. Surprises lurk around every corner.

features

It's hard to avoid clichés when talking about Mexico. It really is a land of contrasts – its people, its climate, its landscape. The majority of Mexicans are *mestizos*, mixed Spanish and Mexican blood, with pure indigenous groups concentrated mainly in the south, in Oaxaca, Chiapas and the Yucatán peninsula. Other pockets are found in Michoacán (Tarascans), in the mountains of Nayarit and Tabasco (Huichols) and in the rugged northern canyons (Tarahumara).

The official language is Spanish, but the most common native language after that is Nahuatl, the ancient langauge of the Aztecs. The large indigenous populations preserve their own language, customs, dress and crafts, and a visit to a local market makes for a memorable experience. Here you will find a fascinating mix of sights, sounds and aromas and an overwhelming variety of produce and crafts.

GEOGRAPHY

- At 1,958,201sq km (755,866sq miles) in area, Mexico is about a quarter of the size of the USA.
- The highest peak is the Pico de Orizaba (5,760m/18,898ft).
- Mexico City lies at an altitude of 2,240m (7,350ft).

- Mexico's coastline totals 10,150km (6,307 miles).
- Mexico is home to nearly 30,000 species of flowering plants, 1,000 species of birds, 2,000 of fish and about 450 of mammals.

SOCIO-ECONOMIC

- Mexico is the most populous Spanish-speaking country in the world.
- The population is approximately 109 million, with between 20 and 30 million inhabiting the capital.
- The indigenous population is estimated to be nearly 30 million.
- 56 indigenous languages survive.
- Around 90 percent of Mexicans are Roman Catholics.
- An estimated 45 million Mexicans live in conditions of extreme poverty.
- In 2009, 723,000 Mexicans were arrested while attempting to cross illegally into the USA, the lowest figure since the early 1970s.
- 70 years of PRI (Partido Revolucionario Institucional) rule was ended in 2000 when Mexicans voted overwhelmingly for the National Action Party (NAP).

VARIOUS

- There are 200 or so varieties of chili.
- Of Mexico's tequila exports, 87 percent go to the USA.
- *Pulque*, a pre-Hispanic beer brewed from the maguey plant, still represents about 10 percent of Mexico's total alcohol consumption.

food & drink

Mexican cuisine combines traditional indigenous recipes and ingredients with Spanish and North American influences. As varied as the country's scenery, the food of Mexico covers every budget, from street-corner tacos to sophisticated dishes that are reverting to pre-Hispanic recipes after decades of "international" cuisine.

NATIONAL SNACKS

Corn tortillas have been the staff of life for centuries and still accompany most dishes, while tacos and burritos are stuffed versions that make filling snacks. Less flavorsome wheat tortillas are now making inroads in the north, while dark-blue or red versions are made from special types of corn. The ubiquitous tacos, sold on every street of the country, are crisp fried tortillas stuffed with a fantastic variety of fillings and often topped with

grated cheese. If you are careful about where you buy them, tacos make delicious and very cheap appetizers. In the south, *tamales* enter the field. These are similar, except that the ingredients are wrapped and steamed in corn husks or banana leaves and may sometimes be sweet. Further variations on the tortilla theme include *enchiladas* (cheese or chicken tacos baked in a spicy sauce) and quesadillas, mainly cheese-filled tortillas. A common accompaniment to the above is *frijoles*, red beans in a mushy sauce.

TIMING

To get the most out of Mexican cuisine, follow the Mexican's rhythm. This entails large breakfasts that include fresh fruit and eggs – try *huevos rancheros*, fried eggs and diced chili in a tomato sauce atop a tortilla. Mexican coffee, apart from in the coffee-growing region of Veracruz, is generally a diluted affair, so real aficionados should order espresso – Italian-style coffee is available in most upscale restaurants. Tea is also a pale imitation of the real thing, but Mexicans make up for this with a fantastic selection of fresh fruit juices *(jugos de frutas)*, and you can order your own combination.

The main meal in Mexico is lunch, eaten at any time between 2 and 5pm, when restaurants offer good-value set menus (*comidas corridas*). Dinner, if taken at all, is generally after 9pm. Tourists who may not want a large lunch will find that resorts cater to European eating hours, but if you travel off the beaten track you will find only upscale restaurants open in the evenings.

SEAFOOD

Mexican seafood is best along the coast, and resorts cook up exceptionally fresh fish such as *huachinango* (red snapper), *robalo* (snook) and *camarones* (prawn) dishes. However, be warned, *sopa de camarón* is one of Mexico's spiciest dishes. Freshwater fish include *pescado blanco*, a delicate white fish from Lago de Pátzcuaro, and *langostino*, a large crayfish usually cooked *al mojo de ajo*. This popular seafood preparation consists of fried garlic – again, be warned!

short break

If you only have a short time to visit Mexico and would like to take home some unforgettable memories, you can do something local and capture the real flavor of the area. The following suggestions will give you a wide range of sights and experiences that won't take long, won't cost very much and will make your visit very special.

- **Stretch out on a Pacific beach** under a shady *palapa* at Huatulco, Puerto Vallarta, or Puerto Escondido, or swim with pelicans and whales in Baja California.

- **Explore a less-visited** archaeological site such as Yagul (➤ 62) to soak up pre-Hispanic history without the crowds.

- **Admire the prowess** of a baroque masterpiece and the fertile imagination of its sculptors in Taxco, Puebla, Cuernavaca, Querétaro, or Oaxaca.

• **Take a boat** tour on a lagoon to observe Mexico's rich bird life, both native and migratory, at San Blas (➤ 137).

• **Get a close-up** of one of Mexico's seismic giants: Popocatépetl, neighboring Iztaccíhuatl (➤ 73), Pico de Orizaba, Mexioc's highest peak, or the Cofre de Perote, near Xalapa.

• **Explore the markets** of towns such as Pátzcuaro (➤ 95) or Oaxaca (➤ 148–152), where the craft work is outstanding, then tour the surrounding villages to observe craftspeople at work.

• **Go scuba diving or snorkeling** at Cozumel (➤ 176) or Isla Mujeres (➤ 177) in the company of technicolored tropical fish.

• **Indulge in countless varieties** of tequila at the Plaza Garibaldi in Mexico City, while being serenaded by *mariachi* sounds. Do the same thing in Guadalajara (➤ 92), where the *mariachis* have their origins, or in Veracruz (➤ 159), where the *marimba* joins the band.

- **Steep yourself in colonial history** in Mexico City's Centro Histórico, paying homage to the last remnants of the proud Aztec culture at the Templo Mayor (➤ 89), before retreating to a restaurant to sample pre-Hispanic cuisine.

- **Visit an indigenous village** in Chiapas, such as San Juan Chamula (➤ 156), to see a unique synthesis of ancient Maya worship and Catholic rituals.

Planning

Before you go

WHEN TO GO

Cancún

JAN	FEB	MAR	APR	MAY	JUN	JUL	AUG	SEP	OCT	NOV	DEC
23°C	23°C	25°C	26°C	27°C	28°C	28°C	28°C	28°C	27°C	25°C	24°C
75°F	75°F	78°F	80°F	82°F	84°F	84°F	84°F	83°F	81°F	78°F	76°F

High season   Low season

In Mexico, climate depends as much on altitude as it does on latitude or longitude, so it's difficult to make generalizations. The best time to go is in the dry season, between October and April, but even in the "rainy season" the rains usually only fall for an hour or two every day. In the northern states it tends to stay relatively dry year round. The highlands, including Mexico City, are usually mild, but with sharp temperature differences between day and night.

August is vacation time for Mexicans and rooms can be scarce in some of the more popular resorts. Día de los Muertos (Day of the Dead) celebrations at the beginning of November are a fun time to see the locals enjoying themselves.

WHAT YOU NEED

● Required
○ Suggested
▲ Not required

Some countries require a passport to remain valid for a minimum period (usually at least six months) beyond the date of entry – check before you travel.

	UK	Germany	USA	Netherlands	Spain
Passport (or National Identity Card where applicable)	●	●	●	●	●
Visa (regulations can change – check before you travel)	▲	▲	▲	▲	▲
Tourist Card (this is granted on entry and is required on departure)	●	●	●	●	●
Return Ticket	●	●	●	●	●
Health Inoculations	▲	▲	▲	▲	▲
Travel Insurance	○	○	○	○	○
Driving Licence (national)	●	●	●	●	●
Car Insurance Certificate – pay extra for Collision Damage Waiver	○	○	○	○	○
Car Registration Document	●	●	●	●	●

WEBSITES

www.visitmexico.com
www.mexconnect.com
www.mexonline.com
www.mexicocity.com.mx
www.mexperience.com
www.mexicanwave.com
www.sectur.gob.mx
www.cybercaptive.com

TOURIST OFFICES AT HOME

In the UK

Mexican Tourism Board
Wakefield House
41 Trinity Square
London EC3N 4DJ
☎ 020 7488 9392
Information line: 09065 508917
www.mexicotravel.co.uk

In the USA

Mexican Tourist Board
400 Madison Avenue
Suite 11C
New York
NY 10017
☎ 212/308-2110
www.visitmexico.com

HEALTH INSURANCE

It is essential to take out a reliable travel insurance policy before leaving home as emergency hospital treatment can be very expensive. For minor ailments pharmacists give good advice, or you can contact a local doctor through your hotel.

Mexican dentists have a very good reputation. If you need emergency treatment, ask at your hotel for a recommendation.

TIME DIFFERENCES

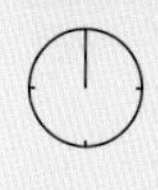

GMT
12 noon

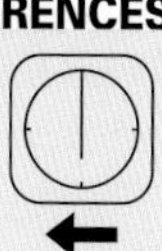

Mexico City
6am

Germany
1pm

USA (NY)
7am

Netherlands
1pm

Spain
1pm

Mexico has four time zones. Most of the country runs on Central Standard Time (6 hours behind GMT). The northern states of Nayarit, Sinaloa, Sonora and Baja California Sur are on Mountain Standard Time (7 hours behind GMT). Baja California Norte is on Pacific Standard Time (8 hours behind GMT). Quintana Roo (Cancún) is one hour ahead of Central Standard Time. All regions change their clocks in April and October.

NATIONAL HOLIDAYS

Jan 1 *New Year's Day*
Feb 5 *Constitution Day*
Mar 21 *Benito Juárez Day*
Mar/Apr *Easter (Maundy Thursday, Good Friday, Easter Sunday)*
May 1 *Labor Day*
May 5 *Battle of Puebla*
Sep 16 *Independence Day (starting eve of 15)*
Oct 12 *Columbus Day*
Nov 1 *All Saints' Day*
Nov 2 *Day of the Dead*
Nov 20 *Revolution Day*
Dec 25 *Christmas*

WHAT'S ON WHEN

January Jan 1*: *New Year's Day.*
Jan 6: *Epiphany* (Three Kings' Day), celebrated with a special cake.

February Feb 2: *Día de la Candelaria* (Candlemas). A family occasion.
Feb 5*: *Constitution Day.* Celebrating the recognition of freedom of speech, the rights of workers and rejection of slavery and discrimination.
Shrovetide Carnivals, above all in Veracruz and Mazatlán.

March Mar 21*: *Birthday of Benito Juárez.* Commemorating the 19th-century statesman who served five terms as president.
Mar 21: *Spring Equinox Festival.* Thousands flock to see the play of light on the pyramid of Chichén Itzá.
Easter (Palm Sunday*, Maundy Thursday, Good Friday and Easter Sunday*). Taxco and the Sierra Tarahumara see the greatest celebrations.
Feria de las Flores (flower festival) in Xochimilco on Easter Sunday.

April Late April to early May – varying dates: *San Marcos National Fair* in Aguascalientes with *mariachis*, bullfights, rodeos.
Mid- to late April: Mexico City Cultural Festival. Art exhibits, drama, concerts and dance staged in venues around the city.

May May 1*: *Labor Day.* A day of peaceful protest to campaign for better working conditions. Many offices, restaurants and banks close.
May 5*: *Battle of Puebla.* Commemorating the Mexican victory over the French army in 1862. The festival is chiefly celebrated in the city of Puebla.
Varying dates: *Cancún International Jazz Festival.*
Varying dates: *Acapulco Music Festival.* Latin bands and solo musicians.

June Varying dates: *Feast of Corpus Christi*. In Mexico City battles re-enacted between Christians and Moors, as well as the *Danza de los Voladores*.
Jun 29: *Tlaquepaque Festival* in Guadalajara.

July Third and last Mon in July: *Guelaguetza Festival* in Oaxaca. Indigenous music and dance.

August Aug 15: *Assumption Day*. Streets of Huamantla, Tlaxcala are carpeted with flower-petal designs.

September Sep 15, 16*: *Independence Day*. Military parades and festivities nationwide. President's *grito* on Mexico City's *zócalo*.
Sep 21: *Autumn Equinox Festival*. Thousands flock to see the play of light on the pyramid of Chichén Itzá.

October Oct 12*: *Día de la Raza* (Columbus Day).
Mid- to late-Oct: *Cervantino Festival* in Guanajuato. An arts festival paying homage to author Miguel de Cervantes, creator of *Don Quixote*.
Fiestas de Octubre in Guadalajara. Month-long celebrations with dance, *charreadas*, food, arts and crafts exhibits.

November Nov 1*: *Día de Todos los Santos* (All Saints' Day).
Nov 2*: *Día de los Muertos* (Day of the Dead). A fusion of pre-Hispanic and Catholic beliefs. Renowned celebrations at Pátzcuaro, Mixquic, Milpa Alta, Iguala. American-style Halloween is now making inroads on Oct 31.
Nov 20*: *Day of the Revolution*. Parades in Mexico City's *zócalo*, and across the country, commemorate the revolution of 1910–20.

December
Dec 12: Festival of Virgen de Guadalupe. Especially celebrated at the Basílica de Guadalupe, Mexico City.
Dec 25*: Christmas Day.

*National holidays when banks and administrative offices close

Getting there

BY AIR

Mexico City Airport

13km (8 miles) to city center

- Train: 35–45 minutes
- Bus: 1 hour
- Taxi: 1 hour

Cancún Airport

16km (10 miles) to city center

- Train: N/A
- Bus: 30–45 minutes
- Taxi: 30–45 minutes

Visitors flying into Mexico have the choice between Mexico City and international airports at beach resorts such as Cancún, Los Cabos, Acapulco or Puerto Vallarta. Guadalajara and Puebla are increasingly popular alternatives. All have money-changing facilities, taxis, restaurants and duty-free shops.

BY LAND

Arriving in Mexico overland from the US is a popular and relatively easy option. There are several border crossings, and you can park your car on the US side and walk across for a day visit. You need Mexican automobile insurance to bring in your own vehicle. Most border crossings have long-distance bus terminals, so you can easily get to your destination from the border. You can also cross by land from Guatemala and Belize.

BY SEA

Cruise ships from all around the world dock in Mexican ports. Destinations such as Acapulco, Cozumel, Ensenada and Puerto Vallarta are popular. Contact a travel agent or website such as www.cruiseweb.com for details and schedules.

Getting around

PUBLIC TRANSPORTATION

Internal flights Domestic air travel in Mexico is not cheap. Aeromexico (www.aeromexico.com) and Aeromar (www.aeromar.com.mx) have the best schedules and deal with bookings for smaller airlines.

Trains Mexico's neglected train service is really only viable for overnight trains from the US border to Mexico City or Guadalajara, or between the two towns. An exception is the spectacular Chihuahua–Pacífico route (➤ 36–37). South of the capital, trains are slow, dirty and dangerous.

Buses The best way to see Mexico on a budget, *primera* (first-class) long-distance bus services use toll roads. They are safer than the second-class buses, which use the secondary roads and are sometimes subject to robberies. Each large town has a *Central Camionera* (bus station) with private lines operating different routes. For longer trips or during public holidays, buy your ticket in advance. Avoid buses where luggage is stowed on the roof.

Ferries The Mar de Cortés has three ferry routes: La Paz–Mazatlán, Santa Rosalía–Guaymas and La Paz–Topolobampo. The Yucatán peninsula has boats from Playa del Carmen to Cozumel, and Puerto Juárez, Punta Sam (car ferry) or Cancún to Isla Mujeres.

Urban transportation Mexico City's metro is excellent and cheap, if a little overcrowded. *Pesero* buses have their destination marked in front, fares are paid to the driver. Elsewhere in Mexico buses and *colectivos* (collective taxis) are easily available, although each city operates different identification systems. Keep small change handy for fares.

FARES AND CONCESSIONS

Students/youths There are few reductions for students, as most youth discounts are for Mexican citizens. Children under 12 get reductions on domestic flights and sometimes free beds in their parents' room.

TAXIS

Mexico City and nearby towns use meters. Elsewhere, a flat fare is charged or price negotiated in advance. Airport taxis and *colectivos* are expensive (fixed fare). Always use official gold and red taxis and check the identity photo on the side of the rear window matches the driver's face. Muggings are not uncommon in unoffical taxis. At night in Mexico City, use radio-taxi services (tel: 55 5519 7690).

DRIVING

- Mexicans drive on the right side of the road.
- Seat belts are compulsory for front seats.
- Breath-testing is not widespread in Mexico but it is not advisable to drink while under the influence of alcohol.
- Widespread drink-driving, hazards such as cattle and speed bumps, and increased vehicular crime make driving at night inadvisable.
- Fuel is Nova (leaded) or Magna Sin (unleaded) and is sold by the liter. Pemex (Mexican fuel) stations are plentiful in central Mexico, but fill up at every opportunity when driving in less populated areas. Payment is in cash. Fuel stations close by 10pm.
- Speed limits are as follows: on highways 110kph (68mph), on country roads 70–80kph (43–50mph) and in towns 40–60kph (25–37mph).
- Contact the Angeles Verdes (Green Angels) for free, on-the-spot technical assistance or tows. Every Mexican state has its own Angeles Verdes Hotline, so it is advisable to obtain this before departure. If your rental car breaks down, phone the rental car company for assistance.

CAR RENTAL

International airports have a large choice of car rental companies. Rates vary considerably. In high season (Dec–Mar) it may be cheaper to reserve from home. A credit card is required to make a deposit. Check the car before signing the contract. Vehicular crime has escalated considerably in the last 10 years and it is not advisable to drive rental cars at night.

Being there

TOURIST OFFICES

SECTUR (Sectaria de Turismo)
Avenida Presidente Masaryk 172,
Bosque de Chapultepec,
11587 Mexico DF
☎ (55) 5250 0123/5250 0151

Baja California Sur
Coordinación General de Turismo,
Carretera Transpeninsular Km 5.5,
Edificio Fidepaz, Apdo Postal 419,
23090 La Paz, Baja California Sur
☎ (612) 124 0100

Chiapas
Secretaría de Desarollo Turístico
Boulevard Belisario Domínguez
950, 29000 Tuxtla Gutiérrez,
Chiapas
☎ (961) 612 4535/613 39396

Guerrero
Acapulco Convention and Visitors
Bureau
Avenue Costera Miguel Alemán
4455, 39850 Acapulco
☎ (744) 484 2423

Oaxaca
Secretaría de Desarollo Turístico
Avenida Independencia 607,
Centro, 68000 Oaxaca, Oaxaca
☎ (951) 515 0717/514 0570

Yucatán
Departamento de Turismo
Calle 59 No 514, Centro, 97000
Mérida, Yucatán
☎ (999) 930 3766

MONEY

The monetary unit of Mexico is the peso ($), divided into 100 centavos. Coins come in 10c, 20c, 50c, $1, $2, $5 and $10 denominations. Notes are in $10, $20, $50, $100, $200 and $500. Major credit cards (particularly Visa and MasterCard) are accepted at large hotels, restaurants, travel agents and stores. ATMs are widespread, even in small towns. International airports all have money-changing facilities with good rates.

POSTAL SERVICES

Correos (post offices) are in every town center and open Mon–Fri 8–6. Overseas mail is slow but generally reliable, and is a better service than internal post. Mail-boxes *(buzón)* are red, but it is safer to post letters at a post office. For anything urgent or of value, use a courier service.

TIPS/GRATUITIES

Yes ✓ No ✗

Restaurants (if service not included)	✓	10–15%
Cafés/bars	✓	10%
Taxis	✗	
Tour guides	✓	5–10%
Porters	✓	US$1–$2
Chambermaids	✓	US$1 per day
Toilet attendants	✓	$1 (peso)

TELEPHONES

If possible, bring your own international phone card from home with an access number for Mexico. Otherwise, Ladatel (long-distance) booths are easily found and operate with phone cards (30 pesos, 50 pesos, 100 pesos) bought at local stores (ask for Telmex cards). Ladatel offices with operators are also widespread. Avoid making long-distance calls from hotels; taxes increase costs. The country code for Mexico is 52.

International dialing codes

From Mexico to:
UK: 00 44
Germany: 00 49
USA and Canada: 00 1
Netherlands: 00 31
Spain: 00 34

Emergency telephone numbers

Police, fire and ambulance: 080
Green Angels (Tourist patrol): (55) 5250 8221
For other crisis lines, see local phone book.

INTERNET SERVICES

WiFi is widely available, with high-speed connections in most upscale resorts and hotels – most include this as complimentary. Internet cafés proliferate in major towns. An hour's usage costs less than US$1.

EMBASSIES AND CONSULATES

UK ☎ (55) 5242 8500; www.ukinmexico.fco.gov.uk/en/
Germany ☎ (55) 5283 2200; www.embajada-alemana.org.mx
USA ☎ (55) 5080 2000; www.usembassy-mexico.gov
Netherlands ☎ (55) 5258 9921
Spain ☎ (55) 5280 4383

HEALTH ADVICE

Sun advice Sunburn is a real hazard. Do not sunbathe between noon and 3pm, always use a high-factor sun cream and wear a hat in exposed areas.

Drugs Prescription and non-prescription drugs are available from pharmacies *(farmacia)*. Bring a basic first-aid kit with you: it should include mosquito repellent, anti-histamine cream for insect bites, a general antibiotic and pain-relief tablets. Anti-malarial treatment need only be taken if traveling extensively in the rainy season (Jun–Sep) near swamps or lagoons.

Safe water and food Never drink tap water. *Agua purificada* (purified water) or bottled water is always supplied in hotels and bottled water is widely available. Drink plenty of water to avoid dehydration. Moctezuma's Revenge (diarrhea) is a common traveler's complaint in Mexico. Avoid eating salads, uncooked or unpasteurized foods (watch out with ice creams) and drinks served with ice, except in decent hotels and restaurants.

PERSONAL SAFETY

Sensible precautions should be taken, above all in larger cities. Pickpockets operate in crowded areas such as markets and bus stations, so do not tempt them by exhibiting jewelry, cameras, or thick wallets. Do not leave valuables lying around in your hotel room; use a safety deposit box. Muggings are on the increase in Mexico City, particularly on unlicensed cabs, so do not carry anything other than essentials. There is, however, a reassurringly high presence of police and security around the central area. Elsewhere, avoid taking solitary walks in remote areas or driving after dark. Drug-related violence since 2006 has taken more than 28,000 lives and looks set to rise. The cities of Juarez, Culiacan and Chihuahua, in particular, are affected by the cartels, though violence is mainly restricted to between gangs and law-enforcement officers.

If anything is stolen, report it for insurance purposes. Avoid taking lifts from new acquaintances unless you are convinced they're trustworthy and beware of seemingly worthy sob stories – most of them are scams.

ELECTRICITY

The power supply is 110 volts. Sockets use two-flat-pin plugs (US style), so Europeans need an adapter and transformer. Most mid- and upper-range hotels have universal outlets for shavers.

OPENING HOURS

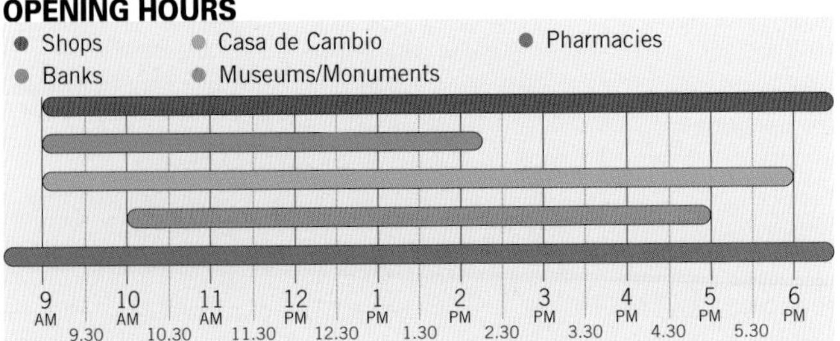

In hotter areas and coastal resorts, shops close at 1 or 2 for lunch, reopening at 4–5pm and finally closing around 9pm. Banks usually open 9am–3:30pm, although certain banks operate longer hours. Post offices open Monday to Friday 8–6. Museums are generally closed on Mondays, and there are regional variations to the opening hours.

LANGUAGE

Spanish is the language used throughout Mexico, although in large resorts English is widely spoken. If traveling to smaller places it is essential to know a few basic phrases. Mexican Spanish has slight differences in vocabulary and usage from Castilian Spanish, but otherwise is very similar. Accents change throughout this vast country, and in some areas you will hear local indigenous languages such as Náhuatl, Maya or Zapotec.

Hello! Good morning	*Hola! Buenos días!*	Please/thank you	*Por favor/gracias*
Good afternoon	*Buenas tardes!*	It's a pleasure	*De nada*
Good night	*Buenas noches!*	I don't speak Spanish	*No hablo español*
Goodbye/see you	*Adiós/hasta luego*	Do you speak English?	*¿Habla inglés?*
Yes/no	*Sí/no*		
Do you have a single/double room?	*¿Tiene una habitación sencilla/doble?*	For two nights	*Para dos noches*
		With fan/air-conditioning	*Con ventilador/aire acondicionado*
With a balcony/sea view	*Con balcon/vista al mar*	Is there a swimming-pool	*¿Hay una alberca?*
How much does it cost?	*¿Cuánto cuesta?/Cuánta se cobre?*	Do you take credit cards?	*¿Accepta tarjetas de crédito?*
Very expensive/cheap/too much	*Muy caro/barato/demasiado*	Where is the nearest bank?	*Dónde esta el banco mas cerca?*
Can I have the menu/bill, please?	*El menu/la cuenta, por favor*	A cup of black coffee/with milk	*Un café americano/con leche*
We'll have two beers please	*Dos cervezas por favor*	Fruit juice	*Un jugo de fruta*
Fizzy mineral water	*Un agua mineral*	A bottle of red/white wine	*Una botella de vino tinto/blanco*
Where is the bus station?	*¿Dónde esta el central camionera?*	How far is the nearest petrol station?	*¿A qué distancia esta la gasolinera mas cerca?*
Straight on/to the left/to the right	*Todo derecho/a la izquierda/a la derecha*	How long is the journey?	*¿Cuánto tiempo dura el viaje?*

Best places to see

1 Barranca del Cobre

Rugged canyons, spectacular waterfalls, old mining villages, Jesuit missions, and the Chihuahua–Pacifico railroad are the highlights of the Copper Canyon.

Five times wider and one-and-a-half times deeper than the Grand Canyon, the 35,000sq km (13,510sq mile) Barranca del Cobre is rapidly becoming a major ecotourism destination. It is composed of five adjoining canyons sliced out of the Sierra Madre Occidental, their sculpted ravines offering startling extremes in climate and vegetation. In winter the upper plateau may be blanketed in snow, while on the canyon floors warm, balmy temperatures prevail; in summer the Sierra Tarahumara is refreshingly cooler than oven-like Chihuahua, though rain is abundant.

The most striking access to this region is by rail, through 88 tunnels and over 39 bridges from Los Mochis, near the Mar de Cortés, to Divisadero and Creel, or arriving in the other less scenic direction from Chihuahua. The main town is Creel. Facilities here include day trips on horseback or by van into the surrounding canyons, to Lago Arareco, Cascada de Cusararé, the hot springs of Recohuata or the six-hour ride to Batopilas, a former silver-mining town 2,000m (6,560ft) below on the canyon floor. In the far north are the thundering waters of the Cascada de Basaseáchic, a 246m (807ft) waterfall whose spectacular pine-clad surroundings are now a national park.

The original inhabitants of this region, the Tarahumara, now only number about 50,000. Their geographical isolation has preserved their distinctive traditions that climax during colorful Easter processions.

✚ 6D 🚆 Daily 1st- and 2nd-class train leaves Los Mochis at 6am, Chihuahua at 7am ✈ Airports at Los Mochis and Chihuahua ❓ Easter processions and dances peak on Good Fri

ℹ Libertad 1300, 1st Floor, Edificio Agustín Melgar, Chihuahua

2 Chichén Itzá

This archaeological site is the most popular in the Yucatán peninsula. Its unique structures are testimony to the sophistication of the Mayan civilization.

Founded in AD514 by a priest, this ceremonial center experienced two peaks, from 600 to 900, and again from the late 10th century until 1196. Civil wars and cultural stagnation followed before Chichén and other northern Maya civilizations finally collapsed in 1441. When the Spaniards arrived a century later, they named the partially ruined structures according to mere supposition.

At the center of the vast plaza in the northern group rises the striking Pyramid of Kukulkán (El Castillo). Its 365 steps and 52 base panels represent the solar year, and twice a year, at the spring and summer equinoxes, the shadows of the north staircase create a serpentine shape that joins the carved snakes' heads at the bottom. To the northwest is a ball court, the largest yet discovered in Mexico, lined with bas-reliefs of players. Overshadowing this is the Templo de los Jaguares (Temple of Jaguars), with extensive jaguar and eagle carvings. Beside it stands the macabre Tzompantli (Platform of Skulls), that once displayed the heads of sacrificial victims.

Across the plaza is the richly decorated Templo de los Guerreros (Warriors' Temple) with, at its base, an extensive, roofless colonnade, the Mil Columnas (Thousand Columns). From the platform high above, the entire plaza is surveyed by a much-photographed *chacmool* (seated human figure).

The highlight of the older group is the Caracol (snail), an elevated circular building once used for astronomical observations. Facing it is the ornately decorated Edificio de las Monjas (nunnery) and, between them, the Iglesia (church), crowned by a remarkable roof comb and adorned with masks of the rain god, Chac.

23H (985) 851 0137 Site and museum: daily 8–6; services: 8am–10pm Expensive; moderate Sun
Cafeteria ($) ADO bus from Mérida, Calle 50
Sound-and-light show nightly: 8pm in Spanish; 9pm in English. Spring and fall equinox celebrations
Tourist information offices in Mérida and Cancún

3 Guanajuato

www.guanajuato.gob.mx

Tumbling down a hillside in central Mexico is this gem of a town. Former silver wealth has left a legacy of superb colonial architecture.

Historically one of Mexico's most important towns, Guanajuato originally earned its status from its rich silver mines, founded in 1546. It never looked back and in 1989 was declared a world heritage site by UNESCO. A network of underground tunnels keeps traffic out of its central plazas and alleys, making it a joy to wander in, though less so to drive in as orientation is not easy.

On a hilltop overlooking the town are the old mines of La Valenciana (one still functions), next to a 1770s church containing three fine baroque altarpieces. Further along the Carretera Panorámica is the Museo de las Momías, another of

Guanajuato's unique sights, containing over 100 mummified bodies retrieved from the local cemetery where they had been impeccably preserved in the mineral-rich soil.

In the town center, the main attraction is the **Alhóndiga de Granaditas,** which houses the regional museum. This imposing building, originally a corn exchange, played a major role in the War of Independence when it became a fortress and later the macabre showcase for the heads of captured rebels. It now exhibits pre-Hispanic objects, altarpieces, religious paintings, and items related to the Independence struggle. A short walk east brings you to the grandiose University, one of the most important in Mexico and, just beyond, the Templo de la Compañia de Jesús, a 1750s church with a remarkable facade. Immediately below is the focal point of town, the lively Jardín de la Unión, backed by the highly decorative Teatro Juárez.

15H Flights from Mexico City
Plaza de la Paz 14; tel: (473) 732 1982

Alhóndiga de Granaditas

Calle 28 de Septiembre (473) 732 1112 Mon–Sat 10–2, 4–6, Sun 10–3

4 Huatulco

www.baysofhuatulco.com.mxi

Situated on what was once a deserted coastline, this fledgling resort offers dramatic scenery and excellent services.

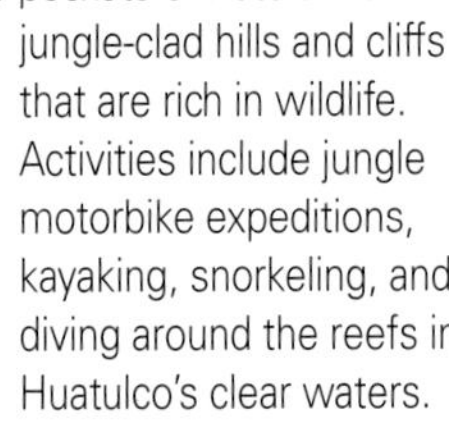

Although Huatulco's string of nine bays was spotted by the Spanish Conquistadors, they were never exploited as a port. It wasn't until the early 1980s that this idyllic fishing village was earmarked by Mexico's resort planners as a follow-up to Cancún. The resort's planners have learned from mistakes elsewhere and built an environmentally sensitive resort with low-rise hotels. Development was stalled by the financial crisis in the mid-1990s. The 2008 US recession also had an impact, as did the outbreak of swine flu the following year.

Today, Huatulco boasts an international airport, over 20 hotels, a marina, an 18-hole golf course and three developed beaches at Tangolunda (the most exclusive), Santa Cruz, and Chahue, as well as a lively inland village, La Crucecita, with budget accommodation. Other beaches remain blissfully untouched. Between the pockets of hotels are jungle-clad hills and cliffs that are rich in wildlife. Activities include jungle motorbike expeditions, kayaking, snorkeling, and diving around the reefs in Huatulco's clear waters.

Although historical sights are totally absent,

Huatulco boasts a modern *zócalo* (main square) at the center of La Crucecita. This animated square is overlooked by a church, **Iglesia de Guadalupe,** worth visiting for its vast contemporary mural of the Virgen de Guadalupe that decorates the entire ceiling vault.

19L Flights from Oaxaca, Mexico City

Santa Cruz, corner Monte Albán, Bahía de Santa Cruz; tel: (958) 581 0176/0177

Iglesia de Guadalupe

Calle Gardenia, La Crucecita Daily 9–8 Cafés and restaurants ($–$$) on plaza

5 Monte Albán

"White Mountain" sits atop a leveled hill above the valley of Oaxaca. Magnificent in scale, layout and setting, the ancient site is an absolute must-see.

Incredible 360-degree views of the barren hills surrounding Monte Albán give a strong sense of proximity to the gods, a fact recognized by the later Mixtecs, who used the abandoned site for offerings and burials between 1350 and the arrival of the Spaniards in the mid-16th century. The ancient Zapotec site was founded around 500BC and peaked between AD500 and 600 with an estimated population of over 20,000. Like many other

Mesoamerican sites, it was abandoned in the eighth century and, apart from its Mixtec interlude, fell into ruin.

From the site entrance and well-designed museum, a path winds uphill to the corner of the northern pyramid, where the breathtaking Gran Plaza opens up before you. To the left is a ball court, a palace, and small temple platforms, and opposite are three large temple structures. Between them a 300m (985ft) plaza unfolds to the majestic steps of the southern pyramid. Other buildings are aligned down the center, yet the overall sense of space remains absolute from any vantage point.

Behind the northern pyramid are five tombs, the most elaborate being Tomb 104. East of this, near the access path, is Tomb 7, source of the fabulous Mixtec treasures displayed in the Museo de las Culturas de Oaxaca in Oaxaca (➤ 149). On the western flank of the plaza, the Palacio de los Danzantes (Palace of the Dancers) was named after a series of carved stone slabs that stand around its base. There are countless theories about these oddly deformed dancing figures.

18L · 6km (4 miles) west of Oaxaca · (951) 516 1215 · Daily 8–5 · Moderate · Café ($) on site · Buses from Oaxaca, Calle Mina 518, every 30 mins 8:30–3:30 · Numerous internal flights to Oaxaca · Sedetur: Independencia, corner García Vigil, Oaxaca; tel: (951) 516 0123

6 Museo Nacional de Antropología

www.mna.inah.gob.mx

This museum is a must for any visitor to Mexico City, as it houses an exemplary display of the nation's indigenous cultures.

Built in the early 1960s, the Anthropological Museum does full justice to the complexities of

Mexico's early civilizations through a dynamic display grouped according to regions. The focal point is a large semi-roofed courtyard fountain; surrounding it are the ground-floor galleries devoted to Mesoamerican artifacts and the upper floor galleries dedicated to the surviving traditions among Mexico's indigenous populations. Another attraction is the museum's location in Chapultepec Park, offering a leafy post-museum walk.

The ground-floor galleries start in the right-hand wing and follow a counterclockwise direction around the courtyard. An introduction to world anthropology and ethnology continues with the origins of the Mesoamericans, before moving into pre-Classic civilizations (1700–200BC). Then follow rooms dedicated to Teotihuacán, Tula (the Toltecs), Méxica (the Aztecs), Oaxaca (Mixtecs and Zapotecs), the Gulf of Mexico (Olmecs, Huastecs and Totonacs), Maya, northern desert cultures, and finally Occidente (the western cultures of Nayarit, Jalisco, and Colima). After visiting some of the archaeological sites covered, the museum collection becomes far more relevant and illuminating.

Highlights include the giant Toltec *Atlante* statue in the Sala de Tula, the Aztec Calendar stone in the spectacular Sala Méxica, and a huge Olmec head from San Lorenzo. Other notable exhibits are the superb Olmec *luchador* (wrestler), the Mayan mask of the Sun God, reproductions of Mayan murals from Bonampak, and a reconstruction of King Pakal's tomb from Palenque.

Ciudad de México 1d Paseo de la Reforma, corner Gandhi, Bosque de Chapultepec, Mexico City (55) 5553 6386/6381 Tue–Sun 9–7 Moderate Café ($) off courtyard Chapultepec Guided tours, audio-guides, bookshop

7 Palenque

Deep in the rainforest of Chiapas stands this superb Maya site, both evocative and historically significant.

Palenque was founded in AD615 by the great Mayan king Pakal, who set out to create a new architectural style. At the center of the main site stands the Palacio (palace), a large complex of courtyards, corridors and tunnels crowned by a tiered tower that was probably an observatory. The entire structure is decorated with relief carvings, stucco friezes, and carved stelae.

Virtually opposite towers the Templo de las Inscripciones (Temple of Inscriptions), where steep steps rise to a summit temple then descend into the extraordinary tomb of King Pakal. Over 620 hieroglyphic inscriptions (including the date of 692) are surrounded by rich stucco decoration. Pakal's carved sarcophagus remains in the crypt but his fabulous jewelry is now at Mexico City's Anthropological Museum (➤ 46–47). Temple XIII, immediately to the west, has revealed the entombed body of the Reina Roja (red queen), adorned with fine jade ornaments that are at the site museum.

Across a stream on the hillside is a group of four beautiful temples. Some distance north lies another distinct group where a ball court fronts the Templo del Conde (Count's Temple). From here a path leads along the stream through jungle and past unexcavated structures to the main road and the museum and crafts shop.

21K (916) 345 0356/0211 Daily 8–5 Moderate Cafeteria ($) in museum *Collectivo* bus to site from Palenque, Calle Allende Airstrip The ruins are in a remote location. If traveling independently take sensible precautions and always travel by day. Avoid traveling by second-class bus as hold-ups on unlit roads are not uncommon Avenida Juárez, corner Absolo, Palenque

8 Taxco

Taxco boasts a spectacular natural setting high in pine-covered mountains and some impressive colonial extravaganzas.

Taxco, a former staging-post on the royal road south to the port of Acapulco, developed considerably in the 18th century thanks to the enterprising French mining magnate José de la Borda, who left his mark both here and in Cuernavaca. A subsequent long and somnolent period ended in the 1930s when the American William Spratling regenerated the silver industry.

Red-roofed, whitewashed houses tumbling down the slopes line a maze of crooked cobblestoned streets winding uphill from the main road to the Plaza Borda. This social and commercial hub is overshadowed by the magnificent church of **Santa Prisca** (1759), a baroque masterpiece that was entirely financed by Borda. No expense was spared; its ornately carved facade and towers house a dazzling interior lined with 12 gilded altarpieces, oil paintings and a monumental organ.

On a tiny plaza behind the church, the Museo Guillermo Spratling exhibits pre-Hispanic artifacts and replicas. A few twisting steps downhill from here stands a museum honoring another of Taxco's illustrious foreign residents, the German explorer Baron von Humboldt, who lived here in 1803. His mansion now houses the Museo de Arte Virreinal, a collection of colonial art with some exceptional pieces. There are numerous other fine mansions and churches to be explored, and a lively market area in the streets below Santa Prisca, packed with silver stores, offers the joys of hard bargaining.

Finally, for panoramic views of the town from the summit of Monte Taxco, take the *teleférico* (cable-car) from Los Arcos, located on the main access road.

16K Easter Week processions peaking on Easter Fri
Avenida de los Plateros 1; tel: (762) 622 6616

Parroquía de Santa Prisca

Plaza Borda (762) 662 0183 Mon–Sat 6am–8pm, Sun 5:30am–9pm Cafés and restaurants ($) on square

9 Teotihuacán

Long before the Aztecs established their capital in central Mexico, Teotihuacán was the dominant center.

An hour's drive from Mexico City, the archaeological site of Teotihuacán ("place of the dead") rises out of dry scrub and cacti. This once magnificent city, that covered over 20sq km (8sq miles) and sustained some 85,000 inhabitants at its zenith, evolved over a period of eight centuries before its destruction around AD750. Controversial 20th-century excavations and restoration of about 80 percent of the structures highlight Teotihuacán's ambitious building, carving and mural techniques.

The site lies a few degrees off a north–south axis traced by the Avenue of the Dead, that ends at the magnificent Pirámide de la Luna (Pyramid of the Moon). At the southern end is the vast Citadel, a walled quadrangle with the Temple of Quetzalcóatl against the eastern wall. This astonishing stepped construction (around AD200), later built over, honors the plumed serpent (Quetzalcóatl) and the rain god (Tláloc) with 366 stone carvings.

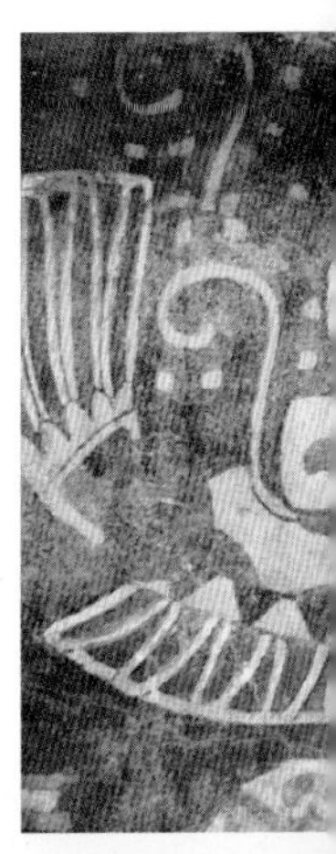

Further north looms the gigantic Pirámide del Sol (Pyramid of the Sun) and, in its southern shadow, a dramatically designed and enlightening new museum displaying priceless exhibits and a huge scale model of the site, crossed by a transparent walkway. At the northwest end of the avenue, flanking another

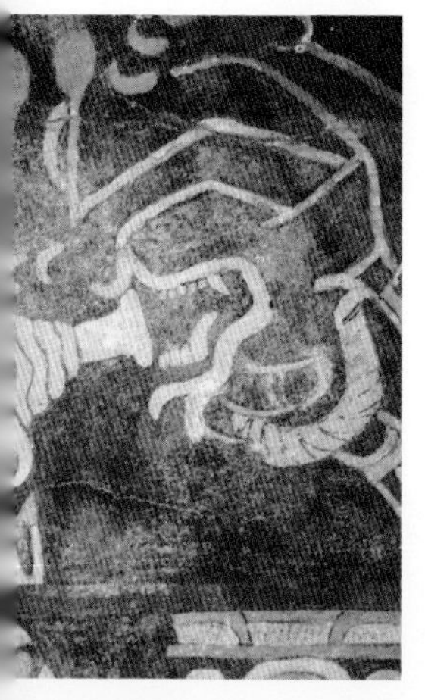

large ceremonial area, stands the extensively restored Palacio de Quetzalpapálotl, part of the priests' residential complex. Here, on an elevated patio, are square columns carved with bird and butterfly designs and remnants of red wall friezes. More patios and lower chambers show depictions of the jaguar god, conch shells and birds. A climb to the summit of the Pirámide de la Luna offers a final, sweeping view of this once great city.

17J (55) 5956 0052 Daily 7am–6pm Moderate Restaurant ($) opposite the Citadel Pirámides' bus from Terminal Tapo San Lázaro Guided tours from Mexico City (through hotels, travel agents)
SECTUR: Avenida Presidente Mazariyk 172, Polanco, Mexico City

10 Xochimilco

Xochimilco is a throwback to the capital's Aztec origins, with its canals and "floating" nursery gardens.

On the far southern edge of Mexico City, weekends are an excuse for feasting on fresh air while cruising the verdant canals of Xochimilco to the insistent tunes of *mariachis*. Brilliantly decorated, pole-propelled *trajineras* (Mexican gondolas), packed with large groups or families, combine with countless flower- and food-sellers in

canoes to create watery traffic jams. Colorfully chaotic, it is a quintessentially Mexican experience.

The tradition of "floating" gardens goes back to the Aztecs, who, due to a shortage of farmland, devised a method of creating islands rooted by willow trees. These *chinampas* were used to grow fruit, vegetables and flowers to supply Tenochtitlán, the capital.

Xochimilco covers an area of 135sq km (52sq miles) that includes the town itself, with its beautiful 16th-century church of San Bernardino de Siena, beside several others, an archaeological museum, and the Parque Ecológico, an extensive area of grasslands, lagoons and canals. This is an ideal destination for birdwatchers, families or anyone desperate for unpolluted air close to the city center.

Xochimilco's final offering is a fascinating private **museum** housed in an atmospheric 400-year-old hacienda. The vast landscaped grounds are an added draw. Named after its owner, Dolores Olmedo, the museum exhibits an important collection of paintings by Diego Rivera and his wives, Frida Kahlo and Angelina Beloff, as well as pre-Hispanic artifacts (some probably copies) and an impressive collection of folk art.

17J Moderate Tren Ligero: La Noria, from Tasqueña Fixed boat prices at Embarcadero
Two-hour tours available (in Spanish) of Parque Ecológico; tel: (55) 5673 8061/7890 or in English through travel agents

Museo Dolores Olmedo Patiño

Avenida México 5843, La Noria (55) 5555 1221/0891
Tue–Sun 10–6 Pleasant open-air café ($)

Best things to do

Good places to have lunch

Baikal ($$)

One of the best restaurants in Acapulco, this jazz-infused sanctuary is set into a cliff-face overlooking the Bay of Acapulco and is reached down a spiral staircase. Dining here is a truly memorable experience.

Carretera Escénica 16 and 22, Playa Guitarron, Acapulco (744) 446-6845 Daily 7am–2am

La Bella Italia ($)

Enjoy delicious Italian dishes away from shopaholic crowds in a sunny garden courtyard. There is an open kitchen, twice nightly musical show and a reasonable wine list.

Canal 21, Colonia Centro, San Miguel de Allende (415) 152 4989 Daily 1–10:30

Café des Artistes ($$$)

Puerto Vallarta's most vibrant restaurant sees diners eating alfresco under the stars and the jungle canopy of giant strangler fig trees in the lush skirts of the Sierra Madre mountains. Enjoy first-rate French cuisine from a celebrated French chef and excellent service.

Sanchez 740, Puerto Vallarta (322) 222 3228; www.cafedesartistes.com Daily 6–11

Casa Oaxaca ($$$)

Some of the most creative food in southern Mexico is served at this modern, romantic eatery in an atmospheric hacienda setting. Fish is the house specialty. Not to be confused with Casa Oaxaca Hotel's own restaurant.

Constitución 104A, Oaxaca (951) 516 8889; www.casaoaxacaelrestaurante.com Daily 1–11

La Casona ($$)

Head to this beautifully restored mansion in Mérida to enjoy

wonderful Italian cuisine. Settle on the attractive patio or in the garden for cool lunches.

✉ Calle 60 No 434, Mérida ☎ (999) 923 8348

Domingo's Place ($$)

Loreto's premier restaurant, stylish Domingo's has been a crowd-pleaser since it opened over 15 years ago. This popular steak house, reputed to be the best in Baja California, is favored by locals and travelers alike for its hearty food and easy ambience. Head to the patio, order steak cooked to your liking, then sit back and enjoy. The menu also includes seafood options.

✉ Salavatiera 154, Loreto ☎ (613) 135 2445

La Palapa Restaurant and Bar ($$$)

This beachfront Puerto Vallarta restaurant is the stuff of local legend. Once graced by the likes of Richard Burton and Elizabeth Taylor (photographs of whom adorn the walls), today it excels itself with fine international cuisine. It's a great place to come for a romantic, candlelit meal.

✉ Pulpito 103, Puerto Vallarta ☎ (322) 222 5225

Top activities

Cenote diving

Cenote diving in the Yucatán Peninsula is an adventurous way of exploring its many mysterious underwater caverns. Cenote Dive Centre has a wide range of options available as well as reef dives around tropical Tulúm.

✉ Andromeda Ote and Centauro Sur Tulúm ☎ (984) 871 2232

Chihuahua–Pacifico Copper Canyon Train

This spectacular scenic railway connects the Pacific Coast with Chihuahua. Beginning at sea level in Los Mochis and rising to 2,500m (8,200ft), it crosses deep ravines and Mexico's most rugged terrain as it finally descends to Chihuahua City. Book in advance to travel first class.

☎ www.mexicoscoppercanyon.com

Diving off Isla Mujeres

Diving and snorkeling with whale sharks is all the rage in the Caribbean waters at Los Manchones and a host of other places off sleepy Isla Mujeres. Sea Hawk Divers is one of the most reliable outfits

✉ Carlos Lazo (on the road to Playa Norte, Isla Mujeres)

☎ (998) 877 0296; www.isla-mujeres.net/seahawkdivers.diving.htm

Golf at Cabo del Sol

Designed by legendary golfer Jack Nicklaus, Cabo del Sol, Mexico's premier golf course, stretches along the Pacific's beautiful coastline. Club rental and instruction are available.

✉ Cabo San Lucas, Los Cabos ☎ (624) 145 6300; www.cabodelsol.com

Horseback riding

See Baja California's spectacular Sierra de la Giganta or the hills around Oaxaca on horseback with Saddling South.

☎ (800) 398 6200; www.tourbaja.com

Kayak fishing in the Bahía de Banderas

Kayak fishing in Puerto Vallarta's Bahía de Banderas is a breathtaking experience that often brings you into contact with dolphins and migrating humpback whales. Eco Explorers facilitate excellent trips (as well as whale watching, dolphin spotting and snorkeling).

✉ Proa SN local 21, Condominio Marina del Rey, Marina Vallarta, Puerto Vallarta ☎ (322) 221 3257; www.ecoexplorer.com.mx

Parasailing

Parasailing at Acapulco, Ixtapa, Cancún or Puerto Vallarta is a memorable experience and can be enjoyed without booking. More information on this, and other active sports, is available online at www.vallartadiscovery.com.

Swimming with dolphins on Cozumel

Swimming with dolphins is food for the soul. You can get close with these wonderfully friendly animals at Discovery Dolphin, based in Cozumel's Chankanaab National Park.

✉ Carretera Costera Sur, Km 9.5, Cozumel ☎ (998) 193 3360; www.dolphindiscovery.com/cozumel

Whale-watching in Baja California

Every year the gray whale migrates some 9,656km (6,000 miles) from the Bering Sea, between Alaska and Siberia, to birth its young and shelter for the winter in Baja California's Sea of Cortés. Blue, humpback and sperm whales can also be seen. Cabo Adventures offer eco-friendly daily sea safaris on inflatable boats.

✉ Cabo Adventures, Boulevard Paseo de la Marina, Lote 7, Cabo San Lucas ☎ (624) 173 9500; www.cabo-adventures.com

a drive in the Oaxaca Valley

This drive covers the valley southeast of the state capital, taking in craft villages and archaeological sites.

Leave Oaxaca by following signs to Istmo or Tehuantepec, which brings you to Highway 190. You soon enter the village of El Tule, with its colorful church and giant tree.

This gnarled ahuehuete tree is claimed to be the world's largest tree, standing 40m (130ft) high and weighing an estimated 550 tons. It is thought to be some 2,000 years old and is still sprouting.

Continue 6km (4 miles) on the highway to a turn-off on the right to Tlacochuaya.

Here a magnificent church stands within a Dominican monastery complex, its interior notable for ornate floral murals and a 16th-century organ.

Return to the highway, continue east, stopping at the archaeological site of Dainzú before turning left to Teotitlán del Valle, famed for its bright wall-hangings and hand-woven rugs (tapetes). *Return and continue along the highway to another turn-off on the left to Yagul.*

This little-visited Zapotec site sits high in the cactus-studded hills and offers fabulous 360-degree views of the valley. Its ball court is the second largest in Mesoamerica.

Follow the highway to an intersection, take the left fork to Mitla. Drive into the village plaza.

Visit the Frissell Museum before walking uphill past numerous crafts outlets to the red-domed church, crafts market and the superb Zapotec structures (➤ 154).

Continue east from Mitla to a turn-off to Hierve del Agua. An unsurfaced road leads to this sensational site – a petrified mineral waterfall and pools. Return to Oaxaca by the same route.

Distance 120km (75 miles)
Time 5–6 hours, depending on stops
Start/end point Oaxaca ✚ 18L
Lunch Centeotl ($), Zona Arqueológica Yagul; tel 951/562 0289

Best souvenirs

Day of the Dead masks from towns throughout Tlaxcala state

Decorative tinwork and vividly embroidered blouses from Oaxaca

Handblown glass from Tonalá, Guadalajara

Handmade hammocks from Mérida and the rest of the Yucatán

Handwoven textiles from Chiapas and Oaxaca

Jade jewelry from Michoacán

***Laca*, or lacquerware,** from the state of Guerrero

Leather goods from the ranching towns of northern and central Mexico, such as Durango and Zacatecas

Silver jewelry and tableware from Taxco

Talavera ceramics from Puebla or cheaper look-alikes from Dolores Hidalgo

Architectural gems

Capilla del Rosario in Puebla's Santo Domingo (➤ 96)

Catedral Metropolitana in Mexico City (➤ 82)

Palacio de Bellas Artes in Mexico City (➤ 87)

Parroquía de San Miguel in San Miguel de Allende (➤ 100)

Santa Clara and **Santa Rosa** in Querétaro (➤ 97)

Santo Domingo in Oaxaca (➤ 152)

Santo Domingo in San Cristóbal de las Casas (➤ 156)

Santa Prisca in Taxco (➤ 50, 51)

Templo de la Valenciana in Guanajuato (➤ 40)

Best climbs

Iztaccíhuatl, the sister volcano to Popocatépetl, for a close-up on Popo's rising steam (➤ 73).

The church of **Nuestra Señora de los Remedios,** atop the largest pyramid in the Americas at Cholula (➤ 90).

The **Pirámide de la Luna** at Teotihuacán for a clear view of early town-planning (➤ 52, 53).

Take the cable-car up to **Monte Taxco** (➤ 51) for panoramic views of Taxco.

The giant statue of Morelos on the **island of Janitzio** overlooking Lago de Pátzcuaro (➤ 95).

El Faro (the lighthouse) at Mazatlán, the world's second-highest natural lighthouse after Gibraltar (➤ 136).

The dunes at **El Faro Viejo** in Cabo San Lucas, for panoramic ocean views (➤ 123).

Nohoch Mul at Cobá, the tallest pyramid on the northern Yucatán peninsula, for sweeping jungle views (➤ 173).

The **Torre Latinoamericana** in Mexico City: a cheat as you'll be in an elevator (➤ 89).

El Castillo, at the heart of Chichén Itzá (➤ 38–39).

Places to take the children

Acuario Mazatlán

Over 50 aquariums with 200 species of fish from all over the world, performing sea lions, a marine museum and theater.

✉ Avenida de los Desportes 111, behind Motel del Sol, Mazatlán ☎ (669) 981 7815; www.acuariomazatlan.gob.mx 🕐 Daily 9:30–6

Africam

Impressive project that re-creates the environment of Africa to preserve and breed endangered species. Also children's zoo and restaurant.

✉ Carretera Valsequillo, Km 16.5, Puebla ☎ (222) 279 6333; www.africamsafari.com.mx 🕐 Daily 10–6:30 🚌 Bus 72 from, Puebla, Boulevard Heroes del 5 de Mayo

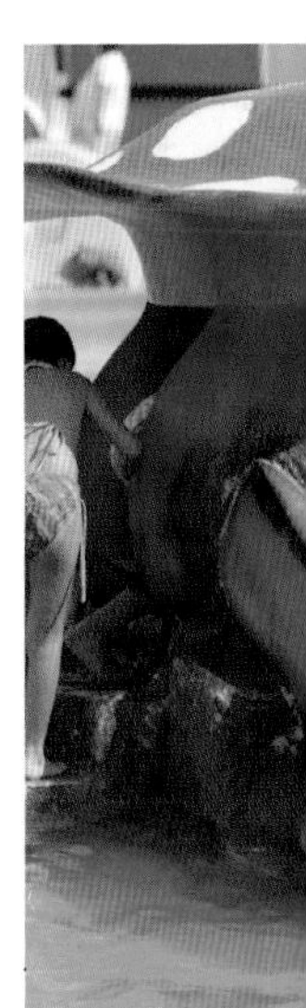

Aquaworld

Cancún's largest watersports centre has an underwater "sub see explorer" that glides through coral reefs for a dry close-up of marine life. Also jungle tours, snorkeling and diving lessons.

✉ Boulevard Kukulcán, Km 15, opposite Melia Hotel, Cancún ☎ (998) 848 8327; www.aquaworld.com.mx 🕐 Daily 6:30am–10pm

CICI

Aquariums, dolphins and water rides keep children more than happy at this well-established park.

✉ Costera Miguel Alemán, Acapulco ☎ (744) 484 8210 🕐 Daily 10–6

Dolphin Discovery

Swim with dolphins on Isla Mujeres. Reservations essential. Minimum age 8 years if accompanied by adult, 12 years if not. Day trips from Cancún, ferry leaves from Playa Langosta.

✉ Playa Langosta, Isla Mujeres ☎ (998) 883 0777/0779 ; www.dolphindiscovery.com 🕐 Four swims daily at 9, 11, 1 and 3

Six Flags Mexico

Southern Mexico City's answer to Disneyland, with over 45 rides, games, a dinosaur show and other attractions.

✉ Carretera Picacho–Ajusto 1500, Mexico City ☎ (55) 5645 0559; www.sixflags.com.mx ⌚ Tue–Thu 10–6, Fri–Sun 10–7 🚇 Taxqueña or Universidad, then taxi

Wet 'n Wild

Toboggans, water slides, waterchutes and several pools for young children. Snorkeling and diving, restaurants, bars and shops.

✉ Boulevard Kukulcán, Km 25, Cancún ☎ (998) 885 1855; www.wetnwildcancun.com ⌚ Daily from 9am

Xcaret

Vast seaside development with manifold attractions – Mayan temples, underground rivers, aquarium, swimming with dolphins, horse-back riding, aviary, butterfly pavilion, orchid farm, museum.

✉ 8km (5km) south of Playa del Carmen, on Highway 307 ☎ (998) 883 3143/883 3144; www.xcaret.com.mx ⌚ Daily 8:30am–10pm

Yumka

Huge jungle and wetlands park with 30-minute boat tour or train through African-type savannah. Good children's attractions.

✉ Camino a Yumka, 16km (10 miles) from Villahermosa ☎ (993) 356 0107; www.yumka.org ⌚ Daily 9–4

Zoológico Miguel Álvarez del Toro

Fabulous zoo where over 200 Central American species roam in large, natural enclosures. Jaguars, quetzals, tapirs, toucans and more on the outskirts of Tuxtla.

✉ Off Libramiento Sur Oriente, Tuxtla Gutiérrez ☎ (961) 614 4701 ⌚ Tue–Sun 9–5

Best natural escapes

Sian Ka'an Biosphere Reserve

Come here to visit the world's second-longest ocean reef, its mangrove-edging savannah home to pumas, white-tail deer, crocodiles, howler monkeys and some 300 bird species. The best way to see the reserve on an organized trek. Contact the conservation-led company Amigos de Sian Ka'an to arrange a visit.

✉ Fuego 2, SM 4 Mza 10, Cancún, Benito Juárez ☎ (998) 892 2958; www.amigosdesiankaan.org

Rio Lagartos and Celestun Biosphere Reserves

In winter, 89 percent of the world's pink flamingoes migrate to these 101,000ha (250,000 acres) of pristine estuaries, mangroves and tropical forests to breed. The area is also home to herons, pumas, ocelots, marsh crocodiles and the endangered hawksbill turtle. Ecoparaiso's one-day trips give a fascinating insight into mangrove and coastal flora and fauna, taking you by foot and boat through the Celestun reserve.

✉ Hotel Eco Paraiso, Municipio de Celestun ☎ 988 916 2100; www.ecoparaiso.com

El Triunfo Biosphere Reserve, Chiapas

Most of Mexico's original rainforest is concentrated around Chiapas, where a high level of rainfall guarantees lush, dense jungle to preserve jaguar, ocelot, parakeet, macaw, toucan and spider monkey populations, as well as tapirs and almost 400 species of bird. It's possible to trek here during the dry months between January and May. Contact Claudia Virgen, the visitors' program coordinator. Prices aren't low but include excellent guides, mules and food. Make reservations well in advance.

✉ San Cristobal 8, Tuxtla Gutiérrez ☎ (961) 125 1122; www.ecobiosfera.org.mx

Centro Mexicano de la Tortuga, Mazunte

In Puerto Angel, near the sleepy village of Mazunte, the Centro Mexicano de la Tortuga (National Mexican Turtle Centre) offers close-up observations of all seven turtle breeds found on the Oaxacan coast, including leatherback, hawksbill, green and Olive Ridley turtles. Research is still carried out here. Guided tours available in Spanish.

✉ Mazunte, Tonameca ☎ 0052 584 3376; www.tomzap.com/turtle.html 🕒 Daily 10–4:30

Volcano Hiking

Two of Mexico's most beautiful volcanoes are found in Popo-Izta National Park, 63km (38 miles) north of Mexico City: Popocatépetl, the country's second largest at 5,426m (17,801ft), and still active, and Iztaccíhuatl, at 5,200m (17,060ft). Most people come for the climbing, but bird-watching and trekking are also popular. Access the national park by car, take a picnic and then to hike to the top of Iztaccíhuatl – well worth the effort for the stunning view of Popocatépetl. Due to its activity in 2005, it is not currently possible to climb Popocatépetl.

At 4,691m (15,390ft) Nevado de Toluca also offers some excellent hiking and climbing. Its crater, which is accessible by car, contains two lakes.

Baja California's Sea of Cortés

Jacques Cousteau described this quiet bay, separated from the Pacific by the Baja peninsula, as the "Galapagos of North America." Sea lions, dolphins, marlin and rays, as well as gray, blue, humpback and sperm whale, congregate in these peaceful waters to give birth to their young and pass the winter. Many tour companies operate sport fishing, kayaking/camping adventures, scuba diving and sea safaris. Los Cabos (► 123) is the main departure point for tours: Visit www.loscabosguide.com for a list of what is available.

Best beaches

Playa de las Ánimas, 19km (12 miles) south of Puerto Vallarta, is a pretty, serene beach near a tiny fishing village where you can get some great fresh seafood.

13J

Playa Delfines, in Cancún's hotel zone on Boulevard Kukulkán near the ruins of El Rey, offers a good view of the turquoise Caribbean.

24H

Playa Hornitos, in central Acapulco, is often overcrowded and thus a little uncomfortable, but it has to be experienced at least once for the high-energy, beautiful people vibe.

16L

Playa Mazunte, 13km (8 miles) west of Puerto Angel, is a stunning stretch of soft sand with a few simple and very tasty seafood joints nearby.

18L

Playa Miramar, 17km (10 miles) south of San Blas, is an isolated beach popular with surfers and seekers of solitude.

13H

Playa Norte, on the northwestern tip of Isla Mujeres and a short walk from the main town, has shallow, calm, turquoise waters that are perfect for a relaxing dip between sunbathing sessions.

24 H

Playa Palancar, on the southeast side of Cozumel, is the resort island's most overlooked beach, with famous off-shore Palancar Reef for diving and a few hammocks hanging under coconut palms inviting an afternoon snooze.

24H

Playa La Ropa in Zihuantanejo, named after a wrecked galleon whose cargo of silk washed ashore, is less than 1,000m (1,100 yards) south of town and perfect for sailing, soccer and chilling.

15K

Tulúm has a tiny cove, 3km (1.5 miles) east of the city center, edged with sugar-white sand and the most perfect turquoise water in the Mexican Carribbean. On the cliffs above the beach stand the fabled ruins of the Mayans. It gets no better than this.

24J

Zipolite, 60km (37 miles) east of Puerto Escondido, is a backpacker's favorite with its cheap accommodations and chilled-out crowd.

18L

Exploring

Traveling through Mexico can be a strangely familiar experience because so much of it has clear European and North American influences. But behind this hybrid facade lies the more secret life of the indigenous people, whose ancestors erected the most incredible pyramids and structures.

Traditional crafts reflect the imagination and flair of the Mexicans, whether intricate handweavings, touchingly crude Tarahumara animal carvings, exquisite ceramics and silverware, or tin *milagros* (votive offerings to saints).

Mexico's magnificent Spanish heritage is one of dazzling baroque masterpieces and grid-like urban layouts, with the inevitable *zócalo* (main square), the social crossroads of every town. In contrast, as the northern border draws closer, there is a distinct feel of growing prosperity and increasing Americanization.

Mexico City and Central Mexico

Guadalajara

Ciudad de México

Central Mexico is the volcano-studded heart of the nation's colonial heritage. It was the silver mines of Zacatecas and Guanajuato that financed countless cathedrals in Spain, while a stream of baroque masterpieces was created in a roll-call of towns from Cuernavaca to Querétaro, Morelia and Puebla.

Today, this is not only one of the most culturally rewarding regions, where interest ranges from local craft specialties to exceptionally designed museums and dramatic archaeological sites, but it also offers spectacular scenery, lakes, forests and generally cooler temperatures. Political events have marked this region – Morelia was the birthplace of José María Morelos, one of the leaders of the Independence movement, and the state of Morelos was the battleground of Emiliano Zapata, the revolutionary hero.

MEXICO CITY

Vibrant, ever-expanding and highly polluted, Mexico City (Ciudad de México) is the political, cultural and economic heart of the country. Rimmed by volcanoes and lying at an altitude of 2,240m (7,350ft), Mexico's capital now claims over 20 million inhabitants and is the third largest city in the world. All of them surrender to the precariousness of living in a city that is sinking into an underground lake, Lago de Texcoco, is plagued by crime and yet survived the terrible earthquake of 1985 with incredible civic solidarity. Yet, despite all its negative factors, no one should pass up on a chance to spend a few days in this stimulating megalopolis.

Mexico City can be divided into three main zones of interest – the Centro Histórico and Alameda area; the Zona Rosa and Chapultepec; and, far to the south, San Angel, Coyoacán and Xochimilco. From Aztec ruins to impressive colonial edifices interspersed with modern blocks and wide boulevards, the city presents strong visual contrasts. On its streets cruises a stream of traffic, dominated by the ubiquitous Volkswagen "beetles", the mainstay of the taxi business. In the Centro Histórico pedicabs offer an alternative form of transport, while the excellent metro system covers the entire city.

Finding your way around can be frustrating, but the streets, alive with color, noise and wandering *mariachi* players, more than compensate for this.

17J

Avenida Presidente Masaryk 172; tel: (55) 5250 0123/5250 0151

Bosque de Chapultepec

This extensive park marks the western limits of the city center and is a favorite with city dwellers for weekend walks, picnics and spontaneous open-air entertainment. Lakes, woods, lawns, museums, an amusement park, a zoo and restaurants are among its diverse offerings. An entire day can easily be spent here.

Crowning the hill is the 1785 Castillo de Chapultepec, which houses the **Museo Nacional de Historia.** Here, a rather dusty display covers Mexican history, and there are murals and the sumptuous royal apartments of the Emperor Maximilian and his wife, Carlota. Don't miss the sweeping views from the terrace café. The castle is reached by a winding path from the Monumento a los Niños Héroes (Monument to the Young Heroes), at the main park entrance, which passes the snail-like Museo del Caracol (covering Independence and the Revolution) on the way.

The star of Chapultepec is the Museo Nacional de Antropología (➤ 46–47), located on the busy Paseo de la Reforma that slices across the park. Nearby are two major art museums – the Museo de Arte Moderno and the Museo Rufino Tamayo (which concentrates on temporary exhibitions of contemporary art). Farther west lies the Jardín Botánico, boating lakes, restaurants, a high-tech children's museum – **Museo del Papalote** – an amusement park and the zoo that claims to be the world's oldest, as it existed during Aztec rule.

Ciudad de México 1e

Museo Nacional de Historia

(55) 5516 2848 Tue–Sun 10–5 Inexpensive; free Sun Café ($) on premises Chapultepec

Museo del Papalote

Avenida Constituyentes, Bosque de Chapultepec (55) 5237 1781 Daily 9–1, 2–6 Constituyentes

Catedral Metropolitana

Dominating the *zócalo*, Mexico City's main historic square, is this massive cathedral (Latin America's largest), which was begun in 1563, although its baroque facade dates from 1681 and the asymmetrical towers and dome were added in 1813. The walls incorporate stones from the ruins of the Aztec Temple of Quetzalcóatl, but far more visible is the gilded baroque of the Capilla de Los Reyes (Chapel of the Kings) that glows in the gloomy interior. Subsidence is an ongoing problem – note the slope from high altar to the entrance – and metal structural supports are unfortunately highly visible. Next door stands the Churrigueresque-style El Sagrario (The Sacred), with a remarkably ornate facade dating from 1760.

Ciudad de México 8c (off map) *Zócalo*, Centro Histórico Daily 7–7 Free Cafés ($) on main square Zócalo

Museo Anahuacalli

This outstanding museum is unfortunately located on the far southern edge of Coyoacán and requires some effort to visit. It was conceived by the renowned

muralist and artist Diego Rivera, who was married to the artist Frida Kahlo in a famously intense relationship, and embodies his identification with Mesoamerican culture. The pyramidal structure houses his collection of 60,000 pre-Hispanic artifacts and a studio where he worked briefly before his death in 1957, leaving some unfinished paintings. Dark, labyrinthine corridors with onyx windows, stone ceiling mosaics, open terraces, arches and stepped, altar-like displays all echo pre-Hispanic forms.

Ciudad de México 4f (off map) Calle del Museo 150, San Pablo de Tepetlapa (55) 5617 4310 Tue–Sun 10–6. Closed Holy Week Moderate; free Sun Taxqueña, then taxi

Museo del Carmen

On the edge of the delightful residential area of San Angel, in a cloistered garden, is this former Carmelite monastery, built in 1617. The attractive, unusual interior encompasses floral friezes, wood and gesso ceiling reliefs, tiles and frescos. Displayed throughout the former chapels and cells is an important collection of baroque religious art and, in the crypt, a somewhat ghoulish line-up of mummies.

Ciudad de México 4f (off map) Avenida Revolución 4, San Angel (55) 5616 2816 Tue–Sun 10–5 Moderate Cafés/restaurants ($–$$) on Plaza San Jacinto San Angel *pesero* bus down Insurgentes

a walk through San Angel

A wander through the relaxed neighborhood of San Angel, along tree-lined cobbled streets, takes in ancient churches, museums and shops.

From the San Angel pesero *bus terminal walk up Avenida Revolución to the Museo del Carmen (► 83) on your right. After visiting this monument, cross the avenue to the Centro Cultural and walk along Calle Madero to Plaza San Jacinto, lined with shops and restaurants.*

On the right-hand side, the 18th-century Casa del Risco offers an unusual ceramic and shell-encrusted fountain, while inside it displays 16th- to 18th-century Mexican and European art. Next door is the Bazar del Sábado, a large crafts market open only on Saturdays. On the far corner of the plaza stands the beautiful 16th-century church and former monastery of San Jacinto.

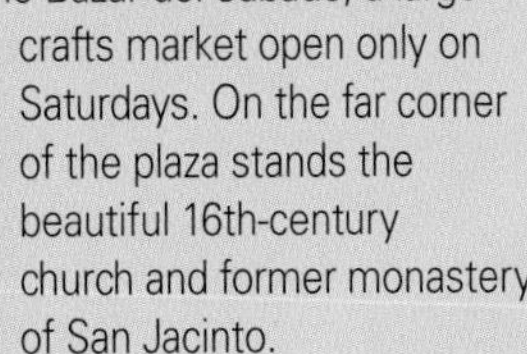

Continue along this street, past the intersection, when it becomes Calle Miguel Hidalgo. At the 17th-century Casa Blanca turn right into Licenciados, following it downhill into Calle Leandro Valle.

These quiet streets offer a classic vision of Mexico City's wealthier residences, often

brightly painted and set behind high walls, in a wide range of architectural styles.

At the main intersection cross Altavista, passing a beautiful 18th-century hacienda on your left (now the San Angel Inn). Opposite stands the Museo Casa Estudio Diego Rivera y Frida Kahlo.

This blue structure was designed by Mexican architect Juan Gorman in 1930 for Rivera and includes a smaller, adjoining structure intended for Frida Kahlo. Rivera's studio, where he died in 1957, gives a fascinating insight into his last years.

Walk east down Altavista to Avenida Revolución and the Museo de Arte Carrillo Gil opposite, before returning south to the bus terminal.

Distance About 3km (2 miles)
Time 2–3 hours, depending on stops
Start/end point San Angel bus terminal
Lunch Restaurant Antigua San Angel Inn ($$$; ➤ 106)

Museo Franz Mayer

In a superbly restored 16th-century mansion, this museum contains an exceptional collection of 16th- to 19th-century fine and applied arts amassed by German immigrant and construction magnate Franz Mayer (1882–1975). Influences and contrasts are highlighted between Asian, Middle Eastern, European and Mexican styles, and priceless exhibits include paintings by Velázquez, Rivera and Zubarán. Inlaid furniture, tapestries, silver and gold objects, wooden sculptures, glass and ceramics complete this impressive collection.

www.franzmayer.org.mx

Ciudad de México 8b Avenida Hidalgo 45, Colonia Guerrero (55) 5518 2266 Tue–Sun 10–5 Moderate Café del Claustro ($) Hidalgo, Bellas Artes

Museo Frida Kahlo

Deep indigo and red-ochre walls picked out with brilliant green window-frames announce the flamboyant tastes of Mexico's foremost woman artist, Frida Kahlo. In the pretty tree-lined streets of Coyoacán, where she spent most of her life, her family home reflects her wide-ranging interests and obsessions, and includes some poignant items such as the wheelchair to which she was confined in her last years, her four-poster bed and her last, unfinished painting (a portrait of Stalin). Beside these is a wealth of memorabilia in which Kahlo's husband, the artist Diego Rivera, figures strongly, alongside her collections of masks, Teotihuacán sculptures, ex-votos, glass, lacquerware and ceramics.

www.museofridakahlo.org.mx
Ciudad de México 4f (off map) Calle Londres 247, Coyoacán (55) 5554 5999 Tue–Sun 10–6 Moderate Cafés, restaurants ($–$$) on Jardín Centenario General Anaya, then taxi

Museo Nacional de Antropología
Best places to see, ➤ 46–47.

Palacio de Bellas Artes
Another of Mexico City's architectural showstoppers presides over the lively park, Alameda Central, on the western edge of the Centro Histórico. The Bellas Artes is a popular cultural center, with excellent temporary exhibitions, a theater where the Ballet Folklórico performs, a bookshop, gift shop, restaurant and a display of murals by Rivera, Orozco and Siqueiros alongside Tamayo, on the upper floors. Set around a vast marble-lined atrium, the interior is pure art deco, in total contrast to the exuberant exterior.

www.bellasartes.gob.mx
Ciudad de México 8c Corner Avenida Juárez and Eje Central, Centro (55) 5512 2593 Palace: daily 10–6; museum: Tue–Sun 10–6 Free Café del Palacio ($$) Bellas Artes Ballet Folklórico: Wed, Sun mornings and Sun evenings

Palacio Nacional

Mexico's first parliament is housed within this vast edifice flanking the eastern side of the *zócalo*. The 17th-century palace replaced two previous ones, and is still the political powerhouse of Mexico as it holds the offices of the President, the National Archives and the Federal Treasury. Above the main entrance hangs the symbolic "Freedom Bell" that rang out in the town of Dolores, on September 15, 1810 to announce the fight for Independence. This is rung annually on the eve of Independence Day by the president to teeming masses gathered in the square.

Inside the courtyard a grand staircase leads up past extensive murals by Rivera, a tour de force that covers the history of Mexico. It is well worth following a guide to have the endless details explained. A small museum on the second floor is dedicated to Mexico's most revered president, Benito Juárez.

Ciudad de México 8c (off map)
Zócalo (55) 9158 1259
Mon–Sat 9–6, Sun 9–2 Free, but bring identification Cafés ($) on *zócalo* Zócalo Military lowering of flag daily before sunset with brass band

Templo Mayor

On the northeastern corner of the *zócalo* (main square) is one of the few Aztec sites that remain. When it was completed in 1487, the temple consisted of seven superimposed structures, each one involving a four-day dedication ceremony and several thousand sacrificial victims. It was unearthed by accident in 1978 during construction of the metro. Four years of excavations uncovered hundreds of superb sculptures, housed in a museum behind the site, designed to resemble the temple layout. Visitors can wander through the temple ruins on raised walkways that give close-ups on the altars devoted to Tláloc, god of rain, and Huitzilopochtli, god of war, along with replicas of sculptures. Highly visible is the wall of skulls in front of the museum, while inside, one of the most outstanding exhibits is a huge carved stone disc depicting the dismembered goddess of the moon, Coyolxauhqui.

Ciudad de México 8c (off map) Seminario 8, Centro (55) 5542 4784 Tue–Sun 9–5 Moderate Zócalo

Torre Latinoamericana

This lofty downtown landmark was the capital's first skyscraper when completed in 1956, but has since been surpassed by others. Towering 139m (456ft), it survived the 1985 earthquake and other tremors due to ingenious anti-seismic foundations that incorporate 361 concrete stilts. Today, it offers the best vantage point for views over the city (on rare, smogless days), particularly breathtaking at night. On the 44th floor is an outdoor viewing deck.

Ciudad de México 8c Corner Avenida Madero and Lázaro Cárdenas (55) 5518 1710 Daily 9:30am–10:30pm Moderate Cafés and restaurants ($–$$) in Centro Histórico Bellas Artes, San Juan de Letrán

Xochimilco

Best places to see, ➤ 54–55.

Central Mexico

CHOLULA

Once a major ceremonial town dedicated to Quetzalcóatl, Cholula suffered extensive destruction by Cortés' army on its march to Mexico City. Numerous shrines and churches include the Convento Franciscano (1549) and the 18th-century Capilla Real with its 49 domes. The Gran Pirámide, the largest pyramid in the Americas, dominates this otherwise nondescript town. Crowning the summit is the 16th-century Templo de Nuestra Señora de los Remedios (Temple of Our Lady of Remedies), while below, some 8km (5 miles) of tunnels have revealed extensive remains of murals. Copies of these are displayed in a museum near the tunnel entrance.

17K

Gran Pirámide

Highway 190, Cholula · Daily 10–5 · Moderate; free Sun · Restaurant Choloyán ($), Avenida Morelos · Guides available to explore main tunnel · Opposite main entrance

CUERNAVACA

Often dubbed the "city of eternal spring," Cuernavaca is a favorite get-away spot for the capital's wealthier inhabitants. Despite a population of over one million, and the largest number of swimming pools per capita in the world, it has a delightful center, and, just 65km (40 miles) south of Mexico City, makes an attractive alternative base. Two adjoining plazas form the heart of town, over which looms the **Palacio de Cortés** (1530), a massive

fortress-palace housing a fascinating museum of regional archaeology, colonial history and the Revolution. There is also a masterful mural by Diego Rivera depicting Spanish oppression of the indigenous peoples.

In front lie the plazas, focal points for a crafts market, promenading and general festivities. A short walk west up Calle Hidalgo brings you to the magnificent Catedral (1530), built by the Franciscans. Although one of Mexico's oldest churches, its interior is strikingly modern. Across Avenida Morelos is the Jardín Borda, a beautiful landscaped garden surrounding a mansion (1783) built by French silver magnate José de la Borda, at one time the richest man in Mexico and later a patron of fine architecture. It was once a favorite retreat for Emperor Maximilian. Historical documents, folk art and temporary art shows are among the exhibits.

17K

Avenida Morelos Sur 187, Colonia La Palma; tel: (777) 318 7561

Palacio de Cortés

Avenida Benito Juárez (777) 312 8171 Tue–Sun 9–6 Moderate

GUADALAJARA

Mexico's second-largest city offers a compact historical center and lively traditions from *mariachis* to glass-blowing. The monuments are dotted around four central plazas surrounding the Catedral, a massive edifice that combines numerous architectural styles. Flanking the Plaza de Armas outside is the Palacio Nacional, where Miguel Hidalgo declared an end to slavery, an event captured by Orozco's powerful murals on its walls.

Immediately north is the **Museo Regional de Jalisco** (1701) housed in a former seminary. Exhibits cover pre-Hispanic artifacts, religious and colonial paintings, decorative arts and handicrafts by Jalisco's Huichol and Cora Indians. To the east stands the neo-classical Teatro Delgollado, where Guadalajara's state orchestra and Grupo Folklórico perform. From here, the Plaza Tapatía stretches east to the impressive Instituto Cultural Cabañas. This is the focal point for the city's cultural activities, as well as housing a homage to José Clemente Orozco, the city's renowned 20th-century painter, whose vigorous murals adorn the domed chapel.

Other offerings include a labyrinthine crafts and food market, the Mercado Libertad and the Plaza de los Mariachis.

Don't miss Tlaquepaque and Tonalá, now engulfed by the urban sprawl. Tlaquepaque makes a colorful outing by bus from the center. Elegant 19th-century mansions converted into restaurants and crafts boutiques radiate from the Jardín Hidalgo and El Parián. Nearby lies Tonalá, with its glass and pottery workshops.

14J

Monumento Los Arcos, Avenida Vallarta 2641, Zona Minerva; tel: (333) 616 9150; Mon–Sat 9–7

Museo Regional de Jalisco

Corner Avenida Hidalgo and Liceo (33) 3614 9957 Tue–Sat 9–5:30, Sun 9–5 Moderate

GUANAJUATO

Best places to see, ➤ 40–41.

LAGO DE CHAPALA

Celebrated for its crimson sunsets and golden dawns, Mexico's largest inland body of water lies on the border between Jalisco and Michoacán states. Its warm climate has attracted a stream of expatriates, from writers such as DH Lawrence and Sybille Bedford to today's 6,000 North American retirees. Sleepy fishing villages stud the lake shore, but the main action is along the northwest shore at Chapala, Ajijic and Jocotepec. Boat trips visit the two islands of Los Alacranes, home to the lake's most scenic fish restaurants, and Mexcala. More authentic in style, and the source of colorful handwoven *serapes* (shawls), is Jocotepec.

14J 50km (31 miles) southeast of Guadalajara, 40 mins by car
In Guadalajara (► 92)

MORELIA

The uncontested architectural jewel of fertile Michoacán is its capital, Morelia, a dynamic yet compact university town. Founded in 1541 as Valladolid, it was renamed Morelia at independence to honor José María Morelos, a native son and key figure in the movement. Dominating the central plaza is a massive pink-stone cathedral, said to be the third largest in the Americas. Harmonious arcades, churches, colleges and imposing colonial buildings radiate from here and include the magnificent mansion that now houses the **Museo Regional Michoacán,** covering local ethnography, archaeology and colonial history. One block north is Mexico's oldest university, the Colegio de San Nicolás, and a few steps farther the superbly proportioned Palacio Clavijero, a majestic example of 17th-century baroque architecture.

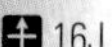 16J

Palacio Clavijero, Nigromante 79; tel: (443) 312 8081

Museo Regional Michoacán

Allende 305, corner Abasolo (443) 312 0407

Tue–Sat 9–7, Sun 9–2 Moderate

PÁTZCUARO

Beside a tranquil lake, Pátzcuaro is an unusual little town. Cobbled streets lined with whitewashed houses wind uphill from Plaza Vasco de Quiroga and Plaza Gertrudis Bocanegra to reach the Basílica de Nuestra Señora de la Salud. Founded in 1554 but rebuilt in 1883, the church contains a much-revered statue of the Virgin of Health, and on the eighth day of every month pilgrims flock here with requests. Close by is the **Museo de Artes Populares,** housed in a former college dating from 1540. Inside are displayed Michoacán's rich local crafts, from lacquerware to copper. Downhill from Plaza Gertrudis Bocanegra is the lake. From the main *embarcadero*, boats ferry visitors to the commercialized island of Janitzio. Crowning its hilltop is a huge statue of independence hero José María Morelos.

15J

Plaza Vasco de Quiroga 50, Guion A; tel: (434) 342 1214

Museo de Artes Populares

Enseñanza y Alcantarilla (434) 342 1029

Tue–Sat 9–7, Sun 9–3 Inexpensive

PUEBLA

Ringed by four volcanoes, including Popocatépetl and Iztacchíhuatl (➤ 73), and less than two hours by road from the capital is Puebla, Mexico's fourth-largest city. Though very industrialized, it is surprisingly easy-going and offers fabulous examples of baroque architecture, in particular the Templo de Santo Domingo. At the heart of this church is the Capilla del Rosario (1690), the most sumptuous Dominican construction in the world, where gilded and carved stucco blankets the dome and walls as a backdrop to a bejeweled figure of the Virgin.

The 17th-century Ex-Convento de Santa Rosa, converted into the Museo de las Artesanías, houses the nuns' kitchens where it is said the famed Pueblan *mole* sauce was invented. Religious art is exhibited at the Ex-Convento de Santa Monica. The former convent is full of disguised doorways and secret passageways, dating from 1857, when President Juárez closed all religious structures.

Flanking the south of the *zócalo* (main square) is the vast Catedral, a mixture of various styles due to its prolonged construction between 1575 and 1649. Three blocks southeast is the impressively designed **Museo Amparo,** where high-tech displays of archaeology and pre-Coumbian art, and examples of colonial furniture are successfully incorporated into a converted 16th-century hospital.

Puebla is noted for the Talavera tiles that adorn many facades or domes. Particularly striking is the Casa de Alfeñique, home to the Museo Regional, while at Uriarte (► 109) workshops still make this renowned decorative ceramic.

17K

Avenida 5 Oriente (southern side of Catedral); tel: (222) 246 2044/1285

Museo Amparo

Calle 2 Sur, corner Avenida 9 Oriente (222) 229 3850 Wed–Mon 10–6 Moderate Museum café ($)

QUERÉTARO

The prosperous, industrial town of Querétaro has a harder edge than its neighbors, yet despite this it is rich in history, with a wealth of baroque architecture and a monumental aqueduct (1735). From the central church of San Francisco, a pedestrian-only area, dense with street stalls, leads uphill to the shady, porticoed Plaza de Armas. This focal point is the site of the 18th-century Government Palace, situated beside several imposing mansions.

Adjoining San Francisco in another former convent is the fabulous Museo Regional, with its renowned collection of viceregal paintings. Southwest from here are Querétaro's two baroque jewels, the Templo de Santa Clara (1633), with walls covered in high-relief altarpieces, and the equally magnificent Templo de Santa Rosa (1752). East of San Francisco stands the church and former Convento de Santa Cruz (1654) that served as a prison for Emperor Maximilian before his execution in 1867.

16J

Plaza de Armas; tel: (442) 238 5073

a drive around Lake Pátzcuaro

Head out of Pátzcuaro on the road to the lake, then follow Highway 14 to Tzintzuntzán, about 20km (12 miles) away.

Above the town is Las Yacatas, a row of stepped, circular pyramids offering sweeping lake views and a small museum. In Tzintzuntzán itself stands the partly ruined 16th-century Templo de San Francisco. Close by are numerous craft outlets for local pottery, woodcarving and straw figures.

Continue to Quiroga, the largest commercial town on the lake. Turn left at the main square for a short drive to Santa Fe de la Laguna.

It was here in the 1540s that Don Vasco de Quiroga, Michoacán's first bishop, attempted to set up a model community based on Thomas More's *Utopia.* The 16th-century hospital and chapel still stand and the village square has been completely renovated, together offering an unusual stop.

Continue to skirt the lake through pine forests to the promontory of Chupicaro.

Next stop is San Jerónimo, a sprawling lakeside village jutting out on a small promontory, where activities concentrate on woodcarving and boatbuilding.

Drive on about 15km (9 miles) to the neighboring villages of Puacuaro, Napizaro and Erongaricuaro.

The pure Purepecha inhabitants of Puacuaro and Napizaro specialize in basket-making. In Erongaricuaro (meaning "look-out tower on the lake") visit the 16th-century Franciscan church and seminary. Handicrafts made here include inlaid furniture, weaving and embroidery.

The road continues around the lake through San Francisco Uricho, Arocutín, Tocuaro and San Pedro, before rejoining Highway 14 and returning to Pátzcuaro.

Distance About 65km (40 miles)
Time Allow a leisurely day to include stops
Start/end point Pátzcuaro 15J
Lunch Restaurants ($) at Chupicaro

SAN MIGUEL DE ALLENDE

This small, picturesque town buzzes with US expatriates, students and visitors. Reflecting this influx is a plethora of cafés, bars, restaurants and stores geared to their needs. Rising above lively Plaza Allende are the lofty, neo-gothic spires of the Parroquía (1880), while across a side street stands the 18th-century birthplace of Ignacio Allende, an independence protagonist. Now the Museo Regional, it illustrates the city's history and archaeology alongside contemporary art. Another impressive 18th-century mansion is the Casa del Mayorazgo; its restored interior now houses an art collection. This artistic theme continues in exhibitions at the Centro Cultural Ignacio Ramírez.

16H

Plaza Allende; tel: (415) 152 6565

EL TAJÍN

Set in lush hills are the magnificent ruins of the Totonac civilization (fourth to 12th centuries). The nearest base is 12km (7 miles) away at the town of Papantla. El Tajín's main sight is the tiered Pirámide de los Nichos (Pyramid of the Niches), incorporating 365 niches, rising beside numerous other buildings and at least 10 ball courts. The main ball-court walls are carved with fine bas-reliefs depicting players, sacrifices and *pulque*-drinking. Uphill lies El Tajín Chico, where more structures surround the Edificio de las Columnas, decorated with intricate stone mosaics. At the entrance, outside the excellent modern museum, a 30m (100ft) pole is used by local *voladores* (flying dancers) to re-enact a dangerous but spectacular Totonac ritual.

18J Highway 130, Estado de Veracruz (25km/15 miles southeast of Poza Rica) (784) 842 0026 Daily 9–6 Moderate Café ($) on site *Voladores* perform daily at noon

TAXCO

Best places to see, ➤ 50–51.

TEOTIHUACÁN

Best places to see, ➤ 52–53.

XALAPA

Blazing sun in the morning and cooler mists in the afternoon characterize Xalapa's picturesque location, high in the coffee-growing hills inland from Veracruz. On the horizon is the Cofre de Perote volcano (4,282m/14,049ft), overlooking this lively university town, with its atmospheric colonial heart of steep, winding streets, gardens, parks and grandiose administrative buildings. The star sight is the excellent **Museo de Antropología,** an imaginatively designed modern building at the northern end of town. Here sunlit patios and terraced marble halls opening onto a landscaped park display a collection of the pre-Hispanic cultures of the Gulf region. Giant basalt heads from the Olmec center of San Lorenzo vie with the wonderful "smiling" sculptures of the Totonacs at El Tajín and the superb pottery of the northern Huastecs.

18J

Boulevard Cristóbal Colon 5; tel: (228) 812 8500

Museo de Antropología

www.xalapa.net/antropologia

Avenida Xalapa, Estado de Veracruz (228) 815 0920 Tue–Sun 9–5 Moderate Cafeteria ($) in museum

HOTELS

CUERNAVACA

Las Mañanitas ($$$)

This restored hacienda is set in beautiful landscaped grounds. The elegant rooms contain Spanish colonial furniture and painting by some of Mexico's finest artists. The considerate, friendly staff will make you feel very welcome. Its restaurant has also been voted one of the best in the world.

Calle Ricardo Linares 107 (777) 314 1466; www.lasmananitas.com.mx

GUADALAJARA

Hotel Frances ($$)

The popular, historic Hotel Frances, dating to 1610, is close to Plaza de la Liberación and is full of Old World charm. Facilities include an inside patio, restaurant and bar. No two rooms are alike.

Maestranza 35 (33) 3613 1190; www.hotelfrances.com

GUANAJUATO

Hotel San Diego ($$)

The San Diego, overlooking the historic town's main square, offers reasonable rooms. Travelers rave about its Italian restaurant.

Jardín de la Unión 1 (473) 732 1300

El Méson de los Poetas ($$)

Sitting on a hillside, this hotel is a great mid-range option, with individually themed rooms named after poets and decent service. Some rooms have kitchenettes.

Positos 35, corner Juan Valle (473) 732 0705; www.mesondelospoetas.com

MEXICO CITY

Best Western Hotel Majestic ($$)

On Madero, the city's most fashion-conscious boulevard, this beautiful baroque hotel sits literally yards from the *zócalo*, with breathtaking views of the cathedral. It offers an insight into colonial taste and history. The terrace restaurant is not to be missed.

Madero 73, Centro (55) 5521 8600; www.bestwestern.com Zócalo

Boutique Hotel de Cortés ($$)
This legendary hotel, reputed to have been the home of the conquistador Hernan Cortés, has stylish, contemporary rooms. Avoid rooms close to the terrace bar, which can be noisy at night.
Hidalgo 85, Centro (55) 5518 2181; www.boutiquehoteldecortes.com
Hidalgo

La Casona ($$$)
This elegant boutique hotel near to the Museum of Anthropology offers stylish rooms and amenities such as a gym and steam bath. The hotel's restaurant has a distinctly French menu.
Durango 280, Condesa (55) 5286 3001; www.hotellacasona.com.mx
Sevilla

NH Centro Historico ($$)
This central, slick, modern hotel offers immaculately clean, spacious rooms. Facilites include a gym and heated outdoor pool.
Palma 42, Centro (55) 5130 1850; www.nh-hotels.com Zócalo

Hampton Inn & Suites Mexico City ($$–$$$)
This stylishly renovated hotel close to the *zócalo* has a contemporary feel. There are two excellent restaurants attached.
Calle 5 de Febrero 24, Centro (55) 8000 5000;
www.hamptonmexicocity.com

MORELIA

Hotel de la Soledad ($$)
This small-scale hotel lies just north of the cathedral. The comfortable rooms surround a peaceful central courtyard.
Zaragoza 90 y Melchor Oca (443) 312 1888

PUEBLA

Camino Real Puebla ($$$)
The sumptuous Camino Real Puebla, a block from the *zócalo*, occupies the former Covento de la Concepción. Rooms have stucco ceilings and are furnished with antiques and colonial-era art.
7 Poniente 105, Centro Historico (222) 229 0909; www.caminoreal.com

QUERÉTARO

Hotel Doña Urraca ($$)

Evoking an atmosphere sympathetic to 16th-century colonial architecture, this luxurious hotel has beautiful chandeliered rooms with hardwood floors, pastel-hued walls and period furniture.

Avenida 5 de Mayo 117 (442) 238 5400; www.donaurraca.com

RESTAURANTS

GUADALAJARA

Cocina 88 ($$$)

With its classically tiled floor and handsome columned interior, Cocina 88 is Guadalajara's premier restaurant. Select your choice of imported Argentine meat from the deli counter or choose from the creative seafood menu, then take your pick from the extensive wine cellar. Eat outside or in the plush interior.

Avenida Vallarta 1342 (33) 3827 5996; www.cocina88.com
Mon–Sat 1:30–1, Sun 2–10

El Sacromonte ($$)

There's a casual atmosphere and excellent Mexican cuisine on offer in this popular neighborhood restaurant. Specialty dishes include *quesadillas cibeles* with rose petals in a strawberry sauce.

Pedro Moreno 1398 (33) 3825 5447 Mon–Sat 1:30–12, Sun 1.30–6

GUANAJUATO

El Gallo Pitagórico ($)

Enjoy the stunning view over central Guanajuato as you dine on Mediterranean cuisine – salads, seafood, pasta (the lasagne is particularly good) and meat with rich sauces.

Constancia 10 (473) 732 9489 Tue–Sun lunch and dinner

Real de la Esperanza ($$)

Best visited at sunset, this diminutive converted chapel is celebrated by diners for its elevated position above town. Enjoy its refined cuisine alfresco while taking in the mountain views.

Carretera Guanajuato-Dolores Hidalgo Km 5, Valenciana (473) 732 1041 Mon–Sat 8:30am–10pm

MEXICO CITY

El Bajio Polanco ($)

A friendly, no-frills place, this restaurant is celebrated for its traditional fare. Service is warm if leisurely but dishes like *chile en nogada* (chilis filled with spicy ground meat and fruits, and topped with a walnut-based sauce) – a seasonal specialty in August and September – and their crab tacos are worth the wait.

Alejandro Dumas 7, Polanco (55) 5281 8245 Daily 8am–11pm Auditorio

El Cardenal ($$)

This sunny terra-cotta hued restaurant is renowned for its fine cuisine with influences from Hidalgo. Enjoy tacos, sweet pastries, great juices and more intrepid dishes.

Palma 23, Centro (55) 5521 8815 Daily 8am–6:30pm Zócalo

La Casa de la Sirenas ($$)

Housed in an atmospheric 17th-century building facing the *zócalo*, with excellent views of the cathedral, this restaurant has alfresco and indoor dining. Expect traditional fare cooked with style and presented beautifully.

Republica de Guatemala 32, Centro (55) 5704 3525 Mon–Sat 11–11, Sun 11–7 Zócalo

Los Girasoles ($$)

Enjoy exquisite Mexican *nouvelle cuisine*, inspired by pre-Hispanic recipes and ingredients, in an elegant setting overlooking Plaza Tolsa. Try the turkey in tamarind *mole* or, if you are feeling more adventurous, one of the more eccentric entries on the menu, such as Mosaico Azteca (worms, ants eggs and crickets). Good service, innovative *mariachis* and a bar complete the picture.

Tacuba 8/10, Centro (55) 5510 0630 Sun–Mon 1–9, Tue–Sat 1–midnight Bellas Artes

Hostería de Santo Domingo ($–$$)

Founded in 1860 and allegedly the oldest restaurant in the city, Santo Domingo is classically Mexican both with its cuisine and

interior decor. Between enjoying heavenly quesadillas and excellent ceviche (raw, marinated fish), check out the mural by Antonio Albanes and the restaurant's famous stained-glass window. This is a favorite with celebrities.
Belisario Domínguez 72, Centro (55) 5526 5276 Daily 10am–10:30pm Allende

Restaurant Antigua San Angel Inn ($$$)
The place to dine in elegant San Angel, this superb 18th-century hacienda serves award-winning international cuisine. Reservations are essential, but the patio also functions as a relaxing bar.
Diego Rivera 50, corner Altavista, San Angel (55) 5616 2222 Mon–Sat 1pm–1am, Sun 1–10 Miguel Allende de Quevedo, then take taxi

MORELIA

Fonda Las Mercedes ($$)
Dine inside or out at this stylish but traditional restaurant in a converted mansion. The international menu includes generous steaks and crepes filled with squash and cheese. The elegant colonial surroundings add luster to this local gem.
León Guzman 47 (443) 312 6113 Mon–Sat 1pm–1am, Sun 1–6

QUERÉTARO

Emilia ($$$)
Enjoy contemporary Italian cuisine to the accompaniment of live music. The menu includes pizzas, homemade pasta and steaks, and there is an extensive wine cellar to whet your palate.
Priv de los Industriales 105 (442) 218 8455 Mon–Sat 1:30–10:30, Sun 8:30–6:30

Restaurant Bar 1810 ($)
Set on the delightful Plaza de Armas and decked in pretty colored lights, this is an excellent place for succulent steaks. The menu also includes fresh seafood and a few pasta dishes.
Anador La Libertad 62 (442) 214 3324 Mon–Sat 8am–midnight, Sun 8am–10pm

SAN MIGUEL DE ALLENDE

La Bella Italia ($)

➤ 58.

Nirvana ($$)

Take a break from Mexican food and enjoy the modern fusion cooking with dishes such as Peking duck with blackberry sauce. The interior design combines water features with plenty of foliage.

Mesones 101 (415) 150 0067 Wed–Mon 8am–10:30pm

SHOPPING

ARTS AND ANTIQUES

Bazar Unicornio

This vibrant weekend market has a cornucopia of high-quality handicrafts: intricately embroidered clothes, papier-mâche figures, masks and blown glass. *Mariachi* music fills the bazaar, as does the redolent aroma of the restaurant inside.

Hernández Macías 80, San Miguel de Allende (415) 152 1306

Casa Poblana

This attractively renovated building in heart of Puebla's antique district, near the Sunday antiques market of Plazuela de los Sapos, sells contemporary home objects (glass, ceramics, wood) beside unusual antiques.

Calle 6 Sur 406, Puebla (222) 242 0848

Plaza San Angel

Mexico City's largest antiques center sells furniture, paintings, decorative arts, silver and bric-à-brac. Weekend market stalls bring the area alive; watch out for copies.

Plaza del Angel, Londres 161 and Hamburgo 150, Zona Rosa, Mexico City
Daily 10–8; antiques market Sat–Sun 10–4 Insurgentes

HANDICRAFTS

Avalos Brothers

The shop has 100 years of glassblowing experience, and you can watch glassblowers at work next to the store. Notice the glass

curtain that divides the shop; it took four years to make. Prices are generally good and their glass caricatures make excellent presents.
✉ Carretones 5, Centro Historico, Mexico City ☎ (55) 5522 5311
🕐 Mon–Fri 10–5

Casa Queretana de Las Artesanías
This state-run shop sells an authentic range of crafts made by local people including bed and table linen, pottery and wooden furniture.
✉ Andador Libertad 52, Centro, Querétaro ☎ (442) 214 1235 🕐 Mon–Fri 11–7, Sat 11–8, Sun 11–4

Casillas Artesanías
Casillas Artesanías sells a good selection of handmade furnishings and handicrafts from the states of Michoacán, Guanajuato, Jalisco, Puebla and Oaxaca.
✉ San Diego 805, Colonia Vista Hermosa, Cuernavaca ☎ (777) 316 3598
🕐 Daily

Cerámica Santa María
Watch the handpainted pottery on sale here being created using techniques and designs developed over 40 years.
✉ Zapata 900, Centro, Cuernavaca ☎ (777) 313 0670

Florería Encanto
This large store has a good selection of reasonably priced pottery from Dolores Hidalgo and glassware from Guadalajara.
✉ Pasteur Sur 29, Querétaro ☎ (442) 212 3737

Fonart
Three branches of this state-run handicrafts store promise top-quality goods. You'll find excellent carved wooden furniture, pottery, ceramics, glass, textiles, jewelry, basket-ware, and more. Shipping can be arranged. Prices are fixed. The largest choice is at Patriotismo branch.
✉ Avenida Patriotismo 691, Mixcoac. Also at Avenida Juárez 89, Centro; Presidente Carranza 115, Coyoacán, Mexico City ☎ (55) 5563 4060
🕐 Mon–Sat 9–9, Sun 10–7 🚇 Mixcoac (main branch)

Gezem

This esteemed colonial-style emporium, selling a range of handicrafts and silverwork, particularly belt buckles, earrings, necklaces, pre-Hispanic-style sculptures and cufflinks, has been in business for 40 years.

✉ Benito Juarez 82, Taxco ☎ (762) 622 7539

Mujeres Productoras

Make your dollar count at this shop selling a vibrant range of handmade crafts, including baskets, shawls, woven handbags, cushions and tablecloths, all made by a local women's cooperative.

✉ Cazada de la Luz 42, San Miguel de Allende ☎ (52) 150 0025; www.globaljusticecenter.org/mujeres_productoras 🕔 Daily 10–5

Uriarte

This renowned workshop and outlet for traditional Talavera ceramics was founded in 1824. It sells exquisitely hand-painted tin-glazed pottery and tiles in rich colors, all made on site.

✉ Avenida 4 Poniente 911, between Calle 9 and 11, Puebla ☎ (222) 232 1598 🕔 Mon–Sat 10–6, Sun 11–6:30

JEWELRY

Bazar del Centro

Pearls and loose semi-precious and precious stones are the specialty at this attractive jewelry emporium.

✉ Isabel la Católica 30, Centro Histórico, Mexico City ☎ (55) 5510 1840 🕔 Mon–Fri 10–7, Sat 10–3 🚇 Pino Suárez

La Bella Elena

Near the Sunday antiques market on Plazuela de los Sapos, this shop sells unusual silver and amber jewelry designs. There is also an upstairs café-bar.

✉ Calle 6 Sur 310, Puebla ☎ (222) 242 0702

Lapidario Barrera

At this Taxco store, designers Salvador Barrera and Lorena Chávez sell their beautifully made Mata Ortíz line of jewelry, which incorporates shards of pottery into finely crafted silver necklaces, bracelets and earrings.

✉ Calle Juan Ruíz Alarcón 3, Taxco ☎ (762) 622 8707

Talleres de los Ballesteros

Jewelry, tableware and other decorative items in sterling silver are sold in this store.

✉ Amberes 24, Zona Rosa, Mexico City ☎ (55) 5511 8281 Ⓜ Insurgentes

MARKETS

Bazar Sábado

This upscale handicrafts bazaar in the southern San Angel neighborhood of Mexico City spills onto the sidewalks. There are few bargains in silver, ceramics, glass, clothing and textiles, although you will find some of the best handicrafts in the country.

✉ Plaza San Jacinto 11, San Angel, Mexico City 🕒 Sat only 10–6 🚌 San Ángel pesero bus down Insurgentes

Casa de las Artesanías

Choose from Michoacán lacquerware, woodcarvings, pottery, copper and furniture at this vast handicrafts emporium housed in a former convent. Shipping can be arranged. There is a small museum on the premises and market stalls in the plaza outside.

✉ Ex-Convento de San Francisco, Plaza Valladolid, Morelia ☎ (443) 312 2486 🕒 Daily 10–3, 5–8

La Ciudadela

Bargaining is essential at this open-air treasure trove selling handicrafts from all over the country. Goods include bracelets, rings, obsidian carvings, ceramics, painted gourds and blankets.

✉ Mercado de las Artesanías, Plaza de la Ciudadela, Calle Balderas, Mexico City 🕒 Mon–Sat 11–7, Sun 11–5 Ⓜ Juárez or Balderas

Mercado Hidalgo

This superb early 20th-century market building in Guanajuato has a food market on the first floor and upstairs stalls selling handicrafts.

✉ Avenida Juárez, Guanajuato 🕒 Daily 7am–9pm

ENTERTAINMENT

Auditiorio Nacional

A major venue, the Auditorio Nacional stages concerts by visiting international rock and pop artists. Check online for details of forthcoming events.

✉ Paseo de la Reforma 50, Mexico City ☎ (55) 9138-1350; www.auditorio.com.mx 🕐 Performance times vary 🚇 Auditorio

Ballet Folklórico

Ballet Folklórico offers a spellbinding panorama of Mexico's diverse traditional dance, music and costumes from Aztec times to today's fiestas. It provides the best opportunity to witness the country's rich performing arts in one fell swoop. Tickets are avilable through hotels or Ticketmaster. Performances take place on Wednesday and Sunday evenings.

✉ Palacio de Bellas Artes, Mexico City ☎ (55) 5512 2593/5521 3633 🕐 Wed and Sun 8:30pm, Sun 9:30am 🚇 Bellas Artes

Bar Mata

Bar Mata, on the third and top-floor terrace of a historic building on the corner of Avenida 5 de Mayo, is a favorite place for late-night drinks.

✉ Filomena Mata 11, corner Avenida 5 de Mayo, Centro Histórico, Mexico City ☎ (55) 5518 0237 🕐 Tue–Sun 8pm–2am 🚇 Bellas Artes

Centro Nacional de las Artes

This arts center has plenty of free events, including contemporary dance, jazz and classical dance.

✉ Avenida Rio Churubusci 79, Mexico City ☎ (55) 4155 0000; www.cenart.gob.mx 🕐 Performance times vary 🚇 General Anaya

La Ópera Bar

This famous haunt, with its moody walnut booths, frosted windows and tiled floors, is a favorite with urbanites and celebrities. Revolutionary hero Pancho Villa left a bullet hole in the ornate tin ceiling back in 1910.

✉ Avenida 5 de Mayo, Mexico City ☎ (55) 5518 7823 🚇 Allende

El Tenampa

As Mexican as it gets, this place on the north side of Plaza Garibaldi is a good place to see the city's famous *mariachi* bands . The music begins after lunch and continues into the small hours.

✉ Plaza Garibaldi, Mexico City 🕐 Mon–Fri until 3am, Sat–Sun until 4am 🚇 Garibaldi

SPORTS AND ACTIVITIES

Africam

➤ 70.

Amigos del Río

This outfit in Xalapa offers white-water rafting at all levels in the lush tropical surroundings of the state of Veracruz.

✉ Calle Chilpancingo 205, Colonia Progreso, 91130 Xalapa ☎ (228) 815 8817

Expediciones México Verde

Experienced white-water rafting agency organizing expeditions all over Mexico. River-rafting season coincides with rains (Jun–Oct).

✉ José Maria Vigil 2406, Colonia Italia Providencia, 44610 Guadalajara ☎ (33) 3641 5598

Fiesta Charra

Mexico's exciting rodeo. The *charread* features horsemanship and lassoing skills.

✉ Rancho del Charro, Avenida Constituyentes 500, Bosque de Chapultepec, Mexico City ☎ (55) 5277 8706 🕐 Sun noon 🚇 Constituyentes

Mexican Wrestling

The Arena Mexico hosts wildly entertaining wrestling bouts on Tuesday and Friday evenings. Expect a passionate local crowd.

✉ Arena Mexico, Dr Lavista 197, Doctores, Mexico City ✉ (55) 5588 0266 🕐 Tue from 7pm, Fri from 8:30pm 🚇 Cuauhtémoc

Six Flags Mexico

➤ 71.

The North and Baja California

Northern Mexico is the land of interminable desert rising abruptly into the Sierra Tarahumara and its canyons (➤ 36–37), while the coastlines are washed by the Pacific Ocean, the Mar de Cortés and, to the east, the Gulf of Mexico. Proximity to the US has generated a string of unattractive industrialized border cities, but in the long finger of land known as Baja California lies a tempting variety of landscapes, from scenic sierra to spectacular, often deserted beaches.

From its border town Tijuana to the southern cape is a distance of 1,200km (746 miles), but it is the southern half that offers the most diversity. This is where whale-watching, bird-watching, sport fishing, scuba diving, riding and trekking take over, backed up by still-fledgling coastal resorts that contrast with remote Jesuit missions in the sierra.

BAHÍA DE LOS ANGELES

This starkly beautiful bay on the Mar de Cortés makes a welcome change from the dry inland desert and is easily reached from the main highway, 68km (42 miles) away. Facilities include an airstrip, several good hotels, RV parks, restaurants and the Museo Naturaleza y Cultura. On the horizon lies Isla Angel de la Guarda, a large island reserve, while the waters of the bay are alive with dolphins, finback whales and sea lions.

3C

BARRANCA DEL COBRE

Best places to see, ➤ 36–37.

CASAS GRANDES

This is the most important archaeological site in northern Mexico, best reached from Ciudad Juárez. Thought to date from AD1000, Casas Grandes (Paquimé) was abandoned in the mid-14th century following attacks by Apaches. Structures on site include platforms, ball courts, underground chambers and the remains of three-story adobe houses. Excavations have unearthed rich finds of Paquimé pottery, necklaces of semi-precious stones and carvings of Quetzalcóatl, some displayed in the museum.

6B Zona Arqueológica de Paquimé, Casas Grandes (636) 692 4140 Tue–Sun 10–5 Moderate Cafeteria ($)

CHIHUAHUA

Capital of Mexico's largest state, Chihuahua prospers thanks to cattle ranches, silver, gold and copper mines, and apple orchards. Drug-related violence in the city is on the increase, but is mainly restricted to members of the drug cartels and law enforcement officers.

The city is the eastern terminus for the Chihuahua–Pacífico railroad (► 36–37), but also offers a number of sights, some linked to Chihuahua's role in the War of Independence and the Revolution (1913). On the central *zócalo* stands the baroque Catedral, and two blocks east is the Palacio Federal, where pro-independence rebel Miguel Hidalgo was imprisoned in 1811 before his execution. Opposite stands the pink Palacio del Gobierno, originally a Jesuit college, with murals depicting Chihuahua's history.

South of the center are two major museums. The **Museo Regional** is housed in the Quinta Gameros, a lavishly decorated mansion displaying art nouveau kitsch and Paquimé pottery from Casas Grandes. It was once the headquarters of the revolutionary hero Francisco "Pancho" Villa. Four blocks south is the **Museo de la Revolución,** in the mansion where he lived. Exhibits include photographs, arms, documents and the black 1922 Dodge peppered with bullet holes in which Villa was assassinated.

7C

Palacio de Gobierno, Plata Baja, Centro; tel: (614) 410 1077

Museo Regional

Quinta Gameros, Paseo Bolivar 401 (614) 429 3300

Tue–Sat 9–1, 3–7

Museo de la Revolución

Calle Décima 3014 (614) 416 2958 Tue–Sat 9–1, 3–7, Sun 10–4 Inexpensive

ENSENADA

Just over 100km (62 miles) south of Tijuana lies Ensenada, Baja California's most popular resort, receiving half a million visitors each year. These are mostly Californians on weekend drinking, eating, shopping and sport fishing sprees, and during the week the town and its bay return to more tranquil fishing and shipping activities. Ultra-fresh seafood is available at the Mercado de Pescas opposite the pier, and local wine can be sampled at the wineries. The largest, **Bodegas Santo Tomás,** offers daily wine tastings in its converted warehouse.

South of town is La Bufadora, a blowhole where wave action produces a dramatic geyser, and the secluded beach of Punta Banda. Nearby are the surfers' favorites of San Miguel, Tres Marías, California and La Joya.

1A

Tourist and Convention Bureau, Lázaro Cárdenas, corner Miramar; tel: (646) 172 3022

Bodegas Santo Tomás

Avenida Miramar 666 (646) 178 3333 Daily tours at 11, 1, 3

Moderate

GUERRERO NEGRO

Although ostensibly a dull town of endless saltflats, vats and warehouses, Guerrero Negro is also the entry point to the Laguna Ojo de Liebre (Scammon's Lagoon), a protected national park where gray whales come to breed between December and March. Lookout posts dot the shore and skiffs can be rented at the beach.

2C Reserva de la Biosfera El Vizcaino: tel: (615) 157 1777/0177; Eco-Tours Malarrimo: tel: (615) 157 0100

HERMOSILLO

The industrialized city of Hermosillo appears to have little charm, yet its strategic site, 225km (140 miles) south of the border town of Nogales on Highway 15, with access to the beach resorts of Guaymas and Bahía Kino, about 100km (62 miles) west, makes it a good stop-over. The attractive colonial heart centers around the shady Plaza de Zaragoza, flanked by the Catedral and the Palacio de Gobierno. South of here lies the Centro Ecológico de Sonora, a zoo and botanical garden full of indigenous and desert specimens.

On the slopes of the Cerro de la Campaña, a hill overlooking the town, is the atmospheric, stone-walled **Museo Regional de Sonora**, in a converted penitentiary. Exhibits here cover Sonora's history from pre-Hispanic times to the present day.

4C

Palacio de Gobierno, Edificio Norte, Paseo Río Sonora; tel: (662) 172 964

Museo Regional de Sonora

Jesús García Finál, corner Estéban Sarmiento (662) 217 1241 Tue–Sat 10–5:30, Sun 9–4 Moderate; free Sun

LA PAZ

The prosperous capital of Baja California Sur (south Baja), La Paz, lies on a large bay opening on to the Mar de Cortés, an ecologically rich gulf dotted with island nature reserves. Protected to the north by the peninsula of El Mogote, whose shores teem with resort hotels, downtown La Paz looks directly west across the bay. This provides a major natural feature – dramatic sunsets.

La Paz (ironically meaning "peace") suffered a turbulent past, set in motion by Hernán Cortés in 1535. Vicious conflicts with the indigenous inhabitants were exacerbated over the centuries by droughts, famines, smallpox, pirates, American troops during the Texan War and, in 1853, the infamous William Walker, intent on installing slavery. As a result, no indigenous groups survived in Baja. The town's fortunes were revived partly thanks to American sport fishermen, ferry services, the Transpeninsular highway and its free-port status, so that today La Paz boasts one of Mexico's highest per-capita incomes.

The center of La Paz radiates from Plaza Constitución, where the Palacio de Gobierno faces the picturesque 19th-century Catedral de la Señora de la Paz, built on the site of a 1720 mission. Close by is the Teatro de la Ciudad, where modern facilities include art galleries and a library. La Paz's history is covered at the **Museo de Antropología,** where informative displays illustrate Baja geology, the early Pericu, Cochimi and Guaicura inhabitants and information on the cave paintings near San Ignacio (➤ 125).

The balmy climate, averaging 25°C (77°F), constant breezes and scenic palm-fringed *malecón* (seafront promenade) make La Paz a relaxing base for exploring the inland sierra, indulging in endless water sports or boat trips, or enjoying the fine white sand of its

beaches. The modernized town center has few historical sights, but Baja is, after all, about the great outdoors.

Although the primary winter (January–March) grounds for humpback whales are around Los Cabos, they sometimes venture into the Bay of La Paz.

Year-round boat trips go to Isla Partida, a seal sanctuary, and the islands of Cerralvo and Espíritu Santo, both nature reserves that offer diving and swimming in the transparent waters of their coves. Sport fishing meanwhile takes advantage of the 850 species of fish in the warm waters of the gulf.

4F

Carretera al Norte Km 5.5; tel: (612) 124 0100. Small office on Tourist Wharf, Paseo Alvaro Obregón 2130, Mon–Sat

Museo de Antropología

Calle Altamirano, corner 5 de Mayo (612) 122 0162 Mon–Fri 8–6, Sat 9–2 Free Cafés and restaurants ($) on Plaza Constitución

a drive through Southern Baja

This drive circles the southern tip of Baja California, passing through dramatic sierra and tiny villages, with a night stop at Los Cabos.

From La Paz drive south on Highway 1 before taking the left fork at San Pedro. From here the road winds up to El Triunfo.

Rich silver veins were discovered here in 1862, leading to a population explosion until the mines closed down in 1926. The town is now virtually a ghost town though small-scale mining has resumed.

Continue 8km (5 miles) to San Antonio, a farming and former silver-mining town, before twisting up into the Sierra El Triunfo. The road descends again to the coast at Los Barriles, renowned for its spectacular winds.

Stop here for a refreshing swim in the Bahía de las Palmas before lunch.

The road skirts the coast before twisting inland and climbing past small villages. About 4km (2.5 miles) beyond Santiago it crosses the Tropic of Cancer, marked by a concrete sphere. At Las Casitas, the road widens to descend to San José del Cabo (➤ 123), an ideal overnight stop. Next morning, head for Cabo San Lucas along the coastal highway and drive to the marina.

Stop here for a glass-bottomed boat trip around the striking rock formation known as El Arco (The Arch).

Drive out of town on Highway 9 to Todos Santos, 80km (50 miles) to the north.

This quiet farming town is attracting a growing community of Americans and a small arts and crafts industry. Beautiful Playa Punta Lobos and Playa San Pedrito are east of town. From here, 80km (50 miles) brings you back to La Paz.

Distance 397km (247 miles)
Time 2 days
Start/end point La Paz ✚ 4F
Lunch Hotel Palmas de Cortés ($$), Conocido en Los Barriles; tel: (624) 141 0050

LORETO

Considered by many archaeologists to be the oldest inhabited site on the Baja peninsula, Loreto is a peaceful getaway in a beautiful setting, backed by the Sierra de la Giganta. The modest town center claims the well-preserved Jesuit mission, from where Father Junípero Serra set out in 1769 to establish a chain of 17 Californian missions. Inside, the **Museo de los Misiones** gives an informative introduction to local missionary activities. Around the church is a pedestrian area leading down to the harbor and beach, where Loreto's few hotels are located. Activities include tennis at one of the world's most modern tennis centers, sport fishing, hiking and scuba diving, as well as boat trips to the lovely Isla Coronado. A mega-resort planned 20km (12 miles) south at Puerto Loreto has been slow to develop, due to strong opposition from local residents and waning enthusiasm from investors – saving this pretty historical town, for the time being at least.

4D

Museo de los Misiones

Salvatierra 16 (613) 135 0005 Tue–Sun 9–1, 3–6 Inexpensive
Cafés ($) in nearby plaza

LOS CABOS

At the tip of Baja lie the twin resorts of Cabo San Lucas and San José del Cabo, 30 minutes apart but quite different in character. Cabo San Lucas is a boisterous, expensive golf resort while San José retains a quaint Mexican village feel beneath its touristic veneer. Los Cabos offer luxury hotels, golf courses, sport fishing, surfing, scuba diving at the unique underwater sand cascades, whale-watching, and horse riding in the sierra.

San José dates back to 1730 when its Jesuit mission was founded. Adjacent Paseo Mijáres, with its stone and stucco 19th-century houses, is now the focal point for restaurants, bars, stores and real-estate agents. At the river estuary, a small **Centro Cultural de Los Cabos** (cultural center) displays arts and crafts, fossils and reproduction cave-paintings, while next to this is an ecological reserve, home to 200 bird species.

The Baja peninsula ends at El Arco, a massive rock arch that terminates the headland. Boat trips from the marina visit this landmark and El Faro Viejo (Old Lighthouse), which offers panoramic views. Pelicans, seals, sea lions, dolphins and whales can be seen. Underwater is a paradise for snorkelers and divers.

5F

Highway 1, Plaza San José, San José del Cabo; tel: (624) 146 9628

Centro Cultural de Los Cabos

Behind Presidente Forum Resort (866) LOSCABOS Tue–Sun 9–5, Wed 9–1 Inexpensive Cafés and restaurants ($$) on Paseo Mijáres

MULEGÉ

Sleepy, low-key Mulegé overlooks the mouth of the 40km (25-mile) Bahía de Concepción, backed by the Sierra de Santa Lucía. The original settlement was founded beside Baja's only navigable river, whose water has nourished large groves of olive trees and date palms. On the hilltop above stands the 1705 Misión de Santa Rosalía, once an open prison and now the Museo de Mulegé, with an eclectic range of exhibits, including old diving and mining equipment. The town mainly attracts sport fishermen, but also offers kayaking upriver or to outlying islands, scuba diving, and jeep or horseback trips to see the Cuevas de San Borjita paintings.

4D Kayaking and cave-painting tours through Hotel Hacienda, Calle Romero Rubio, Mulegé; tel: (800) 346 3942

SAN FELIPE

Running from the border town of Mexicali, Highway 5 ends at San Felipe, a fishing village that has become a resort. The main reason to come here is for the fishing. San Felipe also attracts beach-lovers, as its golden sands border the warm Mar de Cortés (as opposed to the chillier and rougher Pacific). Impressive tides make the beach south of town popular for dune-buggying, and this is

where an increasing number of upscale hotels are appearing.

2A

Mar de Cortés, corner Manzanillo; tel: (686) 577 1155, Tue–Sun 9–2, 4–6

SAN IGNACIO

This attractive oasis town on the edge of the Desierto de Vizcaíno makes a tranquil stop-over as well as being the entry point to Laguna San Ignacio, a major whale-watching spot 70km (43 miles) away. The little town itself has a shady plaza, a mission church (1786), considered by many as one of the most beautiful churches on the Baja peninsula, a small **museum** and date-palm groves planted by the Jesuits. Trips can be arranged to the lagoon during the whale season and all year into the nearby Sierra de San Francisco to see some of the 500 caves painted by the original inhabitants of the area centuries ago (reached by 4WD or on horse- or mule-back only).

3D

Museo Pinturas Rupestres

Misión de San Ignacio

(615) 154 0222

Mon–Fri 8–3 Moderate

HOTELS

CHIHUAHUA

Best Western Hotel Mirador ($$)

This large, modern motel-style hotel is a short walk from the historic heart of the city. Rooms are clean and spacious, if basic.

Avenida Universidad 1309 (614) 432 2200; www.bestwestern.com

Hotel Divisadero Barrancas ($–$$)

Sitting atop the rim of a canyon, this mid-sized hotel enjoys spectacular views taking in Copper, Urique and Tararequa canyons. Rooms are sumptuous and there is a decent café.

Divisadero station, Urique (635) 415 1199; www.hoteldivisadero.com

Quality Inn San Francisco ($$)

Amenities at this modern hotel behind the cathedral include a bar, restaurant and travel desk.

Victoria 409 (614) 439 9000; www.qualityinn.com

CREEL

Best Western The Lodge at Creel ($$)

The timber-clab cabins are exceptionally cozy, with blanket-laden beds and gas fireplaces. The large bar is one of the best in Creel.

Avenida Lopez Mateos 61 (635) 456 0071; www.bestwestern.com

ENSENADA

Best Western El Cid Hotel ($$)

This small hotel has high aspirations with a fine view overlooking Ensenada Bay, a decent swimming pool, WiFi, cable TV, comfortably furnished rooms and helpful bilingual staff.

Avenida López Mateos 993 (646) 178 2401

LA PAZ

Club El Moro ($)

This friendly hotel, across road from the sea, offers air-conditioned rooms with satellite TV and balconies. There is a small pool.

Carretera Pichilingue, Km 2, Colonia Colina del Sol (612) 122 4084; www.clubelmoro.com

Posada de las Flores ($$)
On La Paz's palm-fringed *malecón* (seafront promenade), this colonial-style hotel has been restored with some fine touches. Its rooms have tiled floors, wooden beds and tasteful artwork.
Paseo Obregon 440 (612) 125 5871; www.posadadelasflores.com

LORETO

La Mision ($$)
This colossal colonial-style hotel enjoys fabulous views across the Pacific Baja. It has three enticing restaurants: for sunrise vistas head for breakfast at El Restaurante, or enjoy dinner at the hotel's celebrated Baja Peninsula Restaurant.
Rosendo Robles s/n, Colonia Centro (613) 135 0524

LOS CABOS

Casa del Mar Beach Golf & Spa Resort ($$$)
Somewhat remote, this resort appeals to people seeking seclusion. All the rooms have flatscreen televisions and Jacuzzis. Guests can practise their golf swing at the Cabo Real course or relax in the Sueños del Mar spa.
Carretera Transpeninsular, Km 19.5, San José del Cabo (624) 145 7700; www.casadelmarcabo.com

Casa Natalia ($$)
Set in an oasis of palm trees, waterfalls and lush gardens, and with just 14 comfortable rooms and 2 suites, this is a boutique hotel that truly deserves the name. Its restaurant, Mi Cocina, gets rave reviews. San José's nightlife is also on your doorstep.
Boulevard Mijáres 4, San José del Cabo (624) 146 7100; www.casanatalia.com

Esperanza Resort ($$$+)
Perhaps the most dramatic view of Cabo's famed landmark El Arco is from Esperanza, a plush, luxurious collection of 50 suites and six villas. Located at exclusive and exceptional Punta Ballena.
Carretera Transpeninsular Km 7, Cabo San Lucas (624) 145 6400; www.esperanzaresort.com

RESTAURANTS

CHIHUAHUA

La Casa de los Milagros ($$)

Revolutionary leader Pancho Villa allegedly used to come here. Today, the high-ceilinged, opulently furnished restaurant is just as popular. The succulent steaks are perhaps the best in the city.

Victoria 812 (951) 501 2262 Daily 5pm–late

ENSENADA

El Rey Sol ($$$)

This award-winning restaurant serves French Provençal and Mexican dishes in an elegant, colonial-style setting.

Avenida López Mateos 1000 (646) 178 1733; www.elreysol.com Daily 7–10:30

LA PAZ

La Boheme ($$)

Set in an old traditional house, La Boheme garners glowing reviews for its goat's cheese salad, pizza and decent wine list. Organic food is sourced where possible. Atmospheric, with legions of candles, this is a memorable dining option.

Calle Esquerro 10 (612) 125 6080 Daily 8am–midnight

La Pazta Restaurante ($)

La Paz's favorite Italian, La Pazta serves some wonderful fresh seafood and pasta dishes, as well as terrific lasagne.

Allende 36 (612) 125 1195 Daily 4–11pm

Restaurant La Costa ($–$$)

Restaurants in La Paz are celebrated for their seafood but this one in particular, is renowned for its giant oysters. Sitting by the sea, it draws in the yachting crowd from the nearby marina.

Navarro y Bahia de La Paz (612) 122 8808

LORETO

Domingo's Place ($$)

➤ 59.

LOS CABOS

Damiana ($$)

A colorful, romantic restaurant with patio dining at the heart of San José, Damiana offers sophisticated cuisine, including char-broiled lobster and jumbo prawns. Reservations are recommended.

Paseo Mijáres 8, San José del Cabo (624) 142 0499 Daily 10:30–10:30

Mama Mia ($)

This Neapolitan-style pizza joint has a dizzying range of wood-fired pizzas and calzones on its menu as well as freshly dressed salads and seafood dishes.

Carretera Transpeninsular, Km 29.5, San José del Cabo (624) 142 3940 Daily 8am–10pm

Panchos ($$)

This colorful Mexican restaurant serves hearty traditional dishes and seafood, with tortilla soup, *chile relleno* and lobster among its specialties. There is live music nightly.

Calle Hidalgo, corner Zapata, Cabo San Lucas (624) 143 2891 Daily 6am–11pm

SHOPPING

CLOTHING AND ACCESSORIES

La Sandia

La Sandia stocks stylish women's clothes, accessories and jewelry inspired by pre-Hispanic designs.

Plaza Mijáres 6-B, San José del Cabo (624) 142 2230 Daily 9am–10pm

HANDICRAFTS

Casa Mexicana

On the main square in the upscale resort of Cabo San Lucas, Casa Mexicana sells a wide selection of Mexican handicrafts from Talavera pottery to wooden furniture.

Main plaza, Avenida Cabo San Lucas, Cabo San Lucas (624) 143 1933 Daily 4–10pm

Copal

This attractively converted old house in San José del Cabo sells a fine selection of handicrafts from all over Mexico, including Taxco silver, hand-blown glass, rattan furniture, masks, rugs and pottery.

✉ Plaza Mijáres 10, San José del Cabo ☎ (624) 142 3070 🕐 Daily 9–8

ENTERTAINMENT

Giggling Marlin

This muralled temple of hedonism is a local legend, full of high-jinks drinking and risque dancing, with a well stocked bar.

✉ Corner Matamoros and Boulevard Marina, Cabo San Lucas ☎ (624) 143 1182 🕐 Noon–3am

Tropicana Bar and Grill

A happening place to enjoy live music. The balcony overlooking the stage is the best spot to have a look before you hit the dance floor.

✉ Boulevard Mijáres 30, San José del Cabo ☎ (624) 142 1580 🕐 2pm–3am

SPORTS AND ACTIVITIES

Cabo Adventures

➤ 61.

Cabo Aquadeportes

Scuba diving, equipment rental, instructors.

✉ Hacienda Hotel and Playa Chilena, Cabo San Lucas ☎ (624) 143 0017 or (800) 733 2226

Cabo del Sol

➤ 60.

Chihuahua–Pacifico Copper Canyon Train

➤ 60.

Solmar Fleet

Sport fishing fleet with professional crews and all equipment.

✉ Solmar Hotel Desk, Cabo San Lucas ☎ (624) 143 0646/(800) 344 3349

Acapulco and Pacific Mexico

Acapulco de Juárez

Mexico's oldest beach playgrounds are located along the Pacific coastline between Mazatlán and Acapulco. This is where the country's most dramatic beaches are found, backed by the craggy outline of the Sierra Madre del Sur. Glitzy favorites such as Acapulco and Puerto Vallarta are now joined by Ixtapa-Zihuatanejo, a burgeoning twin resort, and quieter destinations such as San Blas and Barra de Navidad, which offer a more genuine Mexican atmosphere.

Long tracts of coastline remain undeveloped, while short forays can be made inland to hill villages where church bells are the only interruption to a peaceful existence. Water sports are king in these deep blue waters that are sometimes unsuitable for swimming due to their treacherous currents. Acapulco and Puerto Vallarta are the places to go for nightlife, good restaurants and shopping.

ACAPULCO

A stunning sweep of bay led to Acapulco's rise to fame in the 1950s, a revival of its 16th-century fortunes when it was developed by Cortés and his men as a port. In 1565 the first galleon set sail from Manila in the Philippines (then under Spanish rule) to Acapulco, marking the beginning of a flourishing trade route that saw the wealth of the Orient exchanged with that of Nueva España.

With an international airport and a fast toll road from Mexico City, Acapulco's fortunes are assured. Lining its 11km (7-mile) horseshoe bay are endless high-rise hotels, nightclubs, restaurants and a string of beaches where water sports and sun-worshipping set the tone. A concrete jungle or a steamy, sybaritic holiday playground? Opinions are divided, but every visitor is at least won over by the stunning scenery.

From the eastern headland of Playa Bruja, the Costera Miguel Alemán sweeps past a succession of facilities that include five golf courses, children's recreation parks, a crafts market and the San Diego Fort high above the old town, before the bay twists into a peninsula. To the west is the towering cliff of La Quebrada, where daredevil high divers famously plunge into the waves 40m (130ft below, and beyond this lie the tranquil beach and Coyuca Lagoon at Pie de la Cuesta. Air-conditioned buses shuttle along the front, making travel easy. Family holidays are much helped by this excellent infrastructure, but remember that Acapulco is an oasis in one of Mexico's poorest states.

16L

Playa Los Hornos, Costera Miguel Alemán; tel: (74) 844583

Fuerte de San Diego
Overlooking the lively, narrow streets of the old town is this striking stone fort, with panoramic views over the bay and mountains. It was completed in 1617 to protect the thriving port from pirate and buccaneer attacks (including notorious English privateer Sir Francis Drake). Today, it functions as the Museo Histórico, with interesting historical and ethnographic exhibits.

✉ Calle Morelos and Playa Hornitos ☎ (744) 484 4583
🕐 Tue–Sun 9:30–6:30

Isla La Roqueta
A few hundred yards off the Peninsula de las Playas, this small island, reached by glass-bottomed boats from below the Fuerte de San Diego, offers relaxing respite from the main Costera. Cross the island to reach a small, secluded bay with a restaurant, or climb to the lighthouse. The waters are targeted by scuba divers, who come to see the underwater shrine of La Virgen Sumergida.

✉ Off Peninsula de las Playas

Pie de la Cuesta

This 2km-long (1.2-mile), narrow spit of land separating the Pacific from the calm waters of the mangrove and palm-fringed Laguna Coyuca is a favorite with waterskiers and wake-boarders. Sunset fanatics home in on the beach to watch the painted sky from a beach-bar hammock and sponsor daredevil locals to pit their strength against the thundering surf. There are several islands on the lake and a bird sanctuary is to be found on Pajaros.

✉ 11km (7 miles) northwest of Acapulco

La Quebrada

Acapulco's high divers plunge over 40m (130ft) from this cliff into the crashing surf of a narrow cove below. This sight is even more spectacular after sundown, when the last divers carry lighted torches as they plunge. Have dinner or a drink while you witness this carefully timed feat of bravura.

✉ Hotel Plaza Las Glorias, La Mira ⌚ Daily at 1, 7:15, 8:15, 9:15, 10:15pm ✋ Inexpensive

Pacific Mexico

BARRA DE NAVIDAD

This picturesque fishing village developed into an alternative beach resort to soulless Manzanillo, about 60km (37 miles) south. Built on a sandbar next to a large estuary, Barra town offers modest hotels and restaurants, and safe swimming in a scenic setting. Towering above the town is the Grand Bay Hotel, Isla Navidad, with a 27-hole golf course, beach club and a glitzy marina.

13J 60km (37 miles) north of Manzanillo

Jalisco 67; tel: (315) 355 5100

IXTAPA-ZIHUATANEJO

These twin resort towns are only 6km (4 miles) apart, yet have very different characters. Ixtapa is the modern half, its beachfront lined with high-rise hotels squeezed along the long white-sand Playa del Palmar. The wide bay dotted with tiny islands offers boat trips, windsurfing, waterskiing and diving, but swimming can be dangerous. When the waves are strong, head for Isla Ixtapa, where a secluded beach fronts a nature reserve. Ixtapa also offers excursions to lagoons, horse riding, sport fishing, golf and diving.

For some, the former fishing-village setting of Zihuatanejo, with forested headlands plunging into secluded bays, is preferable. Although it is a jazzed-up version of its former self, it offers more atmosphere and older, less pretentious hotels. The least attractive beach, Playa Principal, edges the old town, but beyond a headland to the southeast are Playa Madera, a family beach with economical hotels; Playa la Ropa, home to chic hotels; and Playa Las Gatas, only accessible by boat.

15K Motorboats run all day from Playa Quieta, Ixtapa's northern beach, or sail there with Yates del Sol from Puerto Mio marina

Ixtapa shopping mall; tel: (755) 553 1967

MAZATLÁN

This sprawling resort town is also the largest west coast port between Los Angeles and the Panama Canal, a factor that makes it less commercialized than Mexico's other resorts. Jutting out on a peninsula marked by three hills, its beaches stretch for about 8km (5 miles), lined by a sea-wall promenade, the *malecón*, which ends at El Faro, the headland lighthouse. Behind this hilltop lies the commercial port and old town, while to the far north, Mazatlán's Zona Hotelera monopolizes the seafront.

Despite the influx of tourism, initially attracted by rich sport fishing, Mazatlán still depends on its fishing industry, with tuna-canning factories and shrimp-freezing plants supplied daily by Mexico's largest shrimp fleet. Fish aside, it offers great sports (golf, tennis, riding, water sports), boat trips to two islands with pristine beaches and an atmospheric old town center with a gracious old theater, cathedral and a small archaeological museum.

7F

Edificio Banrural, Avenida Camarón Sábalo; tel: (669) 916 5160

PUERTO VALLARTA

Puerto Vallarta borders Mexico's largest bay, the Bahía de Banderas. It acquired international fame in 1964 when John Huston's film *The Night of the Iguana* hit the screens. At that time Vallarta was just a little fishing village with cobbled streets and tile-roofed houses. Today this aspect still exists (➤ 138–139), as does a moody backdrop of forested hills that sometimes plunge straight into the Pacific, but beyond are high-rise hotels and condos, a marina, hip nightclubs, cosmopolitan restaurants and an array of high-quality stores.

Developments are spreading fast at both ends of the bay, to Mismaloya in the south, where an underwater park lies around the outlying rocks of Los Arcos, and 18km (11 miles) north to the self-contained Nueva Vallarta. Boat trips spirit you to beauty spots such as Boca de Tomatlán, Yelapa, or the Islas Marietas, off Punta Mita. Equally scenic are the roads through the hills, such as to El Tuito; horseback riding or biking are a good alternative to jeeps.

Old Vallarta is still unsurpassed for atmosphere; don't miss the *malecón* boardwalk, with its distinctly surreal sculptures, and the environs of Río Cuale, with its craft markets. An island at the mouth of this river is home to the small **Museo del Cuale**, with interesting displays of ancient clay pottery, as well as restaurants and craft shops, while on its north bank is the *malecón*, town hall and church. The backstreets here are packed with intriguing stores and art galleries. The liveliest town beach, day and night, is Playa Los Muertos, at the southern end of the town center.

13J

Local 18, Zona Comercial, Hotel Canto del Sol; tel: (322) 224 1175

Museo del Cuale

Isla Cuale Tue–Sat 10–3, 4–7, Sun 10–2

SAN BLAS

If you have a good insect repellent and revel in sleepy, unspoiled seaside towns, then this is where to go. Surfing is the number one activity here, closely followed by bird-watching in the mangrove-fringed estuaries and La Tovara lagoon. From November to March over 200 migrating species join the 150 native species. The bay was an important 16th- to 18th-century departure point for Spanish expeditions, and ruins from this period include the old Aduana (Customs House), the hilltop Fuerte de Basilio and a 1769 church.

13H 130km (81 miles) northwest of Puerto Vallarta

Palacio Municipal; tel: (323) 285 0005

a walk in Puerto Vallarta

This walk winds through atmospheric cobbled streets and leads you across the Río Cuale (➤ 137) to where the Mexican heart still beats.

Start at the church on the main square of Old Vallarta.

The curious crown that tops Nuestra Señora de Guadalupe is a replica of the hapless Empress Carlota's crown. It fell off in a 1994 earthquake, but is now perfectly restored.

Leave the church, turn right into Hidalgo and right again up Iturbide. Climb two steep blocks to Carranza and turn right.

At the end of this street on the left is the Callejón de los Tarques, crossed by the bridge that Elizabeth Taylor and Richard Burton built to connect their two houses, known as Casa Kimberley. The house(s) are the stuff of local legend, with actor Peter O'Toole and actor/director John Huston joining Burton regularly for poker games. Under new ownership these houses are being developed into a luxury boutique hotel. There is a lovely view south from the corner.

Return along Carranza as far as Corona. Turn left and walk two blocks downhill for another superb view, looking north. Walk along Matamoros for five blocks, then turn left at Libertad. This goes over the Río Cuale into Insurgentes. Turn left at Lázaro Cárdenas.

On your left is Santa Cruz (built 1902), a popular neighborhood church.

Continue three blocks farther to the Emiliano Zapata market on your right before turning left down Camichín. Climb a few steps at the end to a riverside road. Follow it into Aquiles Serdán and walk straight on, crossing Insurgentes, to Ignacio Vallarta, then turn right. This brings you to steps down on to the Isla Cuale below. Walk west towards the sea.

On your right is the small Museo del Cuale, with an interesting collection of pottery, sculptures and other artifacts from Jalisco, Narayit and Colima.

Distance 3km (2 miles)
Time 2 hours
Start point Nuestra Señora de Guadalupe, Old Vallarta
End point Isla Cuale
Lunch Daiquri Dick's Restaurant/Bar ($–$$), Olas Altas 314; tel: (322) 222 0566

Museo del Cuale
✉ Isla Cuale 🕒 Tue–Sat 10–3, 4–7, Sun 10–2

HOTELS

ACAPULCO

Camino Real Acapulco Diamante ($$$)

All rooms at this full-service, luxury hotel have scenic views of Puerto Marqués Bay. The hotel has a selection of restaurants.
Carretera Escénica, Km 14 (744) 435 1010; www.caminoreal.com

Hotel Elcano ($$$)

The Elcano is opposite the golf course at eastern end of the Costera, with a swimming pool overlooking the beach. Expect spacious rooms, an excellent restaurant, bars and good service.
Avenida Costera Miguel Alemán 75 (744) 435 1500; www.hotelelcano.com.mx

Hotel Las Brisas ($$$)

Located on a mountainside in a residential area, the hotel enjoys excellent views. It is a popular choice with honeymooners.
Carretera Escénica 5255 (744) 469 6900; www.brisashotelonline.com/acapulco_es

IXTAPA-ZIHUATANEJO

Best Western Hotel Posada Real ($$)

This seafront hotel in Ixtapa has air-conditioned rooms, a swimming pool, children's play area, tennis courts, a restaurant and bar. The hotel organizes boat tours to the islands in the bay.
Boulevard Ixtapa (755) 553 0831; http://posadarealixtapa.hotelmx.com

Hotel Dorado Pacifico ($$$)

This spectacular hotel, set in landscaped gardens, enjoys a good beach location. The comfortable rooms have ocean views.
Paseo de Ixtapa sin Lote 3-A (755) 553 2025; www.doradopacifico.com

MAZATLÁN

Hotel Azteca Inn ($$)

Rooms at this friendly hotel are well-furnished and some overlook the pool. Amenities include a bar, coffee shop and parking.
Rodolfo T Loalza 307 (669) 913 1111

Hotel Costa de Oro ($$)

Rooms at this oceanside hotel are arranged around inner patios. Guests can relax in the gardens, take a dip in the swimming pool or dine in the open-air restaurant. Facilities include tennis courts and tours can be arranged.

Camarón Sábalo, Zona Dorada (669) 913 5344; www.costaoro.com

PUERTO VALLARTA

Hacienda San Angel ($$$)

Nine gloriously traditional suites huddle around a hacienda bursting with antique angels, Franciscan doorways, bubbling fountains and hidden atriums at Puerto Vallarta's most exquisite boutique hotel. Part of this complex was once owned by actor Richard Burton.

Miramar 336 (322) 222 2692; www.haciendasanangel.com

Hotel Catedral ($$$)

The hotel is in an attractive art deco-style building, close to the center of Puerto Vallarta and is well positioned opposite the flea market. There are beautiful stylish touches in every room, and excellent views of the cathedral, city center and mountains. Rooms at the top of the building are the best.

Agustin Rodriguez 267 (322) 222 0604; www.hotelcatedralvallarta.com

RESTAURANTS

ACAPULCO

Baikal ($$)

➤ 58.

El Pescador ($$–$$$)

El Pescador is celebrated for its fine sea views and menu, which includes a wide range of fresh seafood and delicious steaks.

Costera Miguel Alemán 1 (744) 469 1234

Tabachin ($$–$$$)

With its upscale ambience and French haute cuisine, Tabachin is a rarefied place to dine. The menu includes lobster medallions with

red peppers and avocado, filet mignon with foie gras, as well as an extensive range of imported wines. In the luxurious Fairmont Pierre Marques resort, this restaurant is highly recommended.
Playa Revolcadero s/n (744) 435 2600 Daily 7pm–12am

MAZATLÁN

Il Mosto ($$)

This much-esteemed restaurant serves typically Greek dishes. The fillet steak sautéed in blackened butter is recommended. Friendly management and alfresco dining make a memorable experience.
Plazuela Machado (669) 985 4366 Daily 1–10pm

El Parador Español ($–$$)

Enjoy Spanish cuisine and seafood specialties in a popular, lively environment. Service here is good.
Avenida Camarón Sábalo, next to El Cid (669) 913 0767; www.elparadorespanol.com Daily 7am–midnight

Señor Frog's ($–$$)

Part of the popular Mexican restaurant chain, Señor Frog's serves a good selection of steaks, soups and well-prepared desserts. The atmosphere gets very lively in the evenings.
Avenida del Mar 882 (669) 985 1110; www.senorfrogs.com Daily noon–3am

El Shrimp Bucket ($$)

For fresh seafood, outdoor dining and great sea views, this restaurant is hard to beat. Try the calamari (squid) – a specialty. Live *marimba* music creates a lively atmosphere in the evenings.
Olas Altas 11 (669) 981 6350 Daily 6:30am–11:30pm

PUERTO VALLARTA

Café des Artistes ($$$)

➤ 58.

La Palapa ($$$)

➤ 59.

Trio Restaurant ($$–$$$)

Enjoy fine European cuisine in a very popular dining spot, in the central part of the city. Sip the generous drinks while listening to live music.

Guerrero 264 (322) 222 2196 May–Oct daily 6–11:30pm; Nov–Apr noon–3:30, 6–11:30pm

SHOPPING

ART AND ANTIQUES

Galería Uno

Selling paintings, sculptures, graphics and posters by well-known Mexican artists, this contemporary art gallery in Puerto Vallarta is housed in an attractive converted house.

Morelos 561, Puerto Vallarta (322) 222 0908 Mon–Sat 10–8

Olinala Gallery

The gallery stocks a well-displayed selection of fine indigenous art, including ritual masks, Huichol beadwork, lapidary work and other rare original pieces.

Lázaro Cárdenas 274, Puerto Vallarta (322) 222 4995 Mon–Sat 10–2, 5–9

Peyote People

This is probably the best place to shop for vivid Huichol art as the owner has direct links with the mountain people who make it, so your money is going to the right place. The quality here is second to none; jaguar heads, skulls and even antlers are all colorfully beaded in ritual symbols.

Juarez 222, Puerto Vallarta (322) 222 2302 Daily 10–8

CLOTHING AND ACCESSORIES

Esteban's

This renowned local designer in Acapulco makes casual and evening wear for men and women to order. A ready-to-wear collection and accessories are also available.

Costera Miguel Alemán 2010, Acapulco (774) 484 3084 Tue–Wed, Fri–Sun 5:30–10pm

HANDICRAFTS

Quetzalcóatl

For indigenous art, such as beaded Huichol pieces, black pottery from Oaxaca, Aztec and Maya reproductions, masks and terra-cotta sculptures, head to this spacious emporium in Puerto Vallarta. Shipping can be arranged.

✉ Juárez 428, Puerto Vallarta ☎ (322) 223 2380 🕒 Mon–Sat 9:30–8:30

Serafina

Wonderfully eclectic, Serafina in Puerto Vallarta sells beautiful embroidered blouses, pashminas, hammered-tin crucifixes and icons, distinctive Mexican handbags, and amber and turquoise bracelets.

✉ Calle Basilio Badillo 260, Viejo Vallarta, Puerto Vallarta ☎ (322) 223 4594 🕒 Daily 10–8

JEWELRY

Albertós

This long-established company in the resort of Zihuatanejo has been designing and selling unique jewelry in gold, silver and precious stones since 1977.

✉ Calle Cuauhtémoc 12 and 15, Zihuatanejo ☎ (755) 554 2161

Taxco Exporta

Choose from a wide selection of silver jewelry from Taxco, including some unique designs. There are some gold pieces and handicrafts on sale, too. Bargaining is necessary.

✉ Calle La Quebrada 315 (opposite diving cliff), Acapulco ☎ (744) 482 7165 🕒 Daily 10am–7pm

ENTERTAINMENT

Baby'O

At this groundbreaking Acapulco nightspot the dance floor is surrounded by tiered spectator seats. Enjoy the latest sound and light equipment and a fast-paced atmosphere.

✉ Costera Miguel Alemán 22, near Hyatt Regency, Acapulco ☎ (744) 484 7474 🕒 Daily 10pm–5am

Club Christine

For a classic mainstream disco head to this Puerto Vallarta club. There's an amazing *son et lumière*. No shorts or flip flops.

✉ Hotel Krystal Vallarta, Zona Hotelera, Puerto Vallarta ☎ (322) 224 6990 🕐 Tue–Sun 10pm–4am

Collage

An entertainment center with billiards and backgammon, video games, sushi bar and dance floor, Collage packs a young crowd of up to 2,000. It's best known for its weekly foam parties.

✉ Calle Proa, at entrance to Marina Vallarta, Puerto Vallarta ☎ (322) 221 0505 🕐 Daily 11am–4am

Hilo

A young crowd and fun atmosphere keep things moving at this cavernously large club. Imposing sculptures tower over the crowd.

✉ Paseo Diez Ordaz 588, Puerto Vallarta ☎ (322) 223 536 1 🕐 Daily 4pm–5am

Palladium

There are stunning views of Acapulco Bay from the glass walls of this popular nightspot, high on a hill. Techno music dominates.

✉ Carretera Escénica Las Brisas, Acapulco ☎ (744) 446 5486 🕐 Daily 10pm–late

Salon Q

Hot tropical sounds keep the rhythm going in this huge dance spot with live bands. Salsa, cumbia, merengue and other Latin beats.

✉ Costera Miguel Alemán 23, near La Palapa, Acapulco ☎ (744) 481 0114 🕐 Daily 10pm–2am

Zoo

Techno, reggae, house and disco music play to a young crowd at central Vallarta's most popular nightspot, easily identified by the giraffe on its roof overlooking the bay. Open dress code.

✉ Paseo Díaz Ordáz 630, Puerto Vallarta ☎ (322) 222 4945 🕐 Daily 10pm–2am

SPORTS AND ACTIVITIES

Acuario Mazatlán

➤ 70.

CICI

➤ 70.

Eco Explorers

➤ 61.

Ecotours de Mexico

This operator offers kayaking, horseback riding, bird-watching, mountain biking, whale-watching and trekking.

✉ Ignacio L Vallarta 243, Puerto Vallarta ☎ (322) 222 6606/222 3310

Pacific Scuba

Diving (PADI certificates) includes night dives, snorkeling at Majahuita beach, Islas Marietas and Los Arcos; whale-watching.

✉ Boulevard Francisco Medina Ascencio 2480, Puerto Vallarta ☎ (322) 209 0364

Vallarta Adventures

Brilliantly organized cruises include snorkeling, kayaking, yoga, hiking, swimming with dolphins and lunch at John Huston's former beachfront home, Las Caletas. Evening cruises include dinner.

✉ Paseo Las Palmas 39A, Puerto Vallarta ☎ (322) 221 0657

Yates del Sol

Yates del Sol, in the resort of Zihuatanejo, organizes speedboat and yacht rental, waterskiing, sunset cruises and snorkeling trips.

✉ Zihuatanejo ☎ (755) 554 2694

Zihuatanejo Scuba Center

The center provides a wide range of diving facilities from beginners to certification courses. Night dives. There is a marine biologist on call for specialists.

✉ Calle Cuauhtémoc 3, Zihuatanejo ☎ (755) 554 2147

Oaxaca and the South

Indigenous people account for over 75 percent of the population in Southern Mexico, giving this region the look of authenticity. Beyond apparently deserted hills are villages with firmly entrenched traditions.

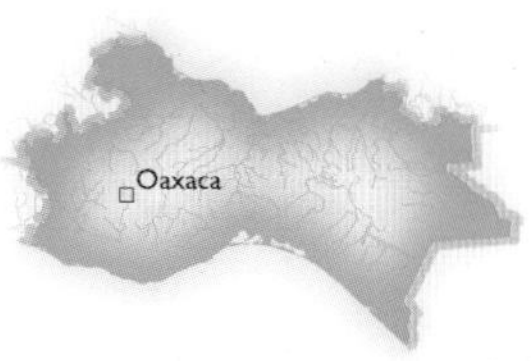

Hugging the coast to the north is the state of Veracruz, with its distinctly tropical, almost Caribbean atmosphere. Oaxaca, to the south, remains queen of history, archaeology, culture and crafts. East of Veracruz is the oil-rich state of Tabasco, once the heart of Mesoamerica's oldest civilization, the Olmecs, but now clearly a front-runner in fast-developing Mexico.

Furthest south is the troubled state of Chiapas, where indigenous people have suffered at the hands of landowners and economic inequality for centuries. This gave rise to the Zapatista rebellion, which began in 1996 and gained a peaceable resolution as recently as 2005. These days Chiapas is a safe place to visit, with people welcoming tourists and the much-needed income that they provide.

In 2005, Hurricane Stan wrought havoc on many coffee-growing estates, washing away an integral part of the region's income and many thousands of lives. Recovery has been slow.

The area boasts high pine-covered mountains, which alternate with tropical rainforests concealing mysterious Mayan ruins.

OAXACA

Oaxaca, capital of the state of the same name, is a graceful, small-scale city. Unique and full of surprises, it is one of Mexico's most colourful towns. History is omnipresent yet not overpowering, while markets, art galleries, craft shops, cafés and restaurants make for endless tempting distractions.

At its heart is the magnificent *zócalo,* rimmed by cafés, and a genuine crossroads for anyone in town. Once the center for the Mixtec and Zapotec civilizations, Oaxaca developed a strong Spanish flavor after it was conquered in 1533. Countless churches (including the masterful Santo Domingo), elegant mansions, government buildings and charming plazas were built, creating a harmonious backdrop for the proud indigenous population.

In 1987, Oaxaca, together with Monte Albán, a fabulous legacy of the Zapotecs (➤ 44–45) was declared a world heritage site by UNESCO. Excellent services, atmospheric hotels and a network of craft villages have been organized and made accessible, offering a wide choice of activities to the visitor. The silhouette of Sierra Madre del Sur is a constant reminder of its rural attractions, whether seen on horseback, bicycle or by car. However, Oaxaca's charm is best enjoyed on strolls along cobbled streets, past brightly painted houses, peeping into churches or courtyards, checking out shops, or people-watching on the *zócalo.*

Oaxaca has endured periods of political unrest, so check the current situation before traveling (www.travel.state.gov.com or www.fco.gov.uk).

✚ 18L

ℹ SECTUR, Juarez 703; tel: (951) 516 0123, www.oaxaca.travel; daily 8–6

Museo de las Culturas de Oaxaca

Next door to Santo Domingo is the former Dominican monastery that now houses the regional museum, backed by a newly landscaped botanical garden. The rooms and vaulted cloisters of this building display the wealth of archaeological artifacts found in the state. Pride of place goes to the fantastic collection of Mixtec jewelry found in Tomb 7 at Monte Albán, including gold, turquoise, rock crystal, jade and silver.

✉ Ex-Convento de Santo Domingo, Alcalá ☎ (951) 516 2991 🕒 Tue–Sun 10–8 💰 Moderate; free Sun

Museo Rufino Tamayo

Rufino Tamayo (1899–1991), one of Mexico's foremost 20th-century painters and a native of Oaxaca, spent over 20 years collecting pre-Hispanic antiquities, and this select museum is the result. Five color-coordinated rooms display some exceptional pieces, in particular those devoted to the Olmec, Occidente, Totonac and Maya cultures. Concerts and art exhibitions are also held here.

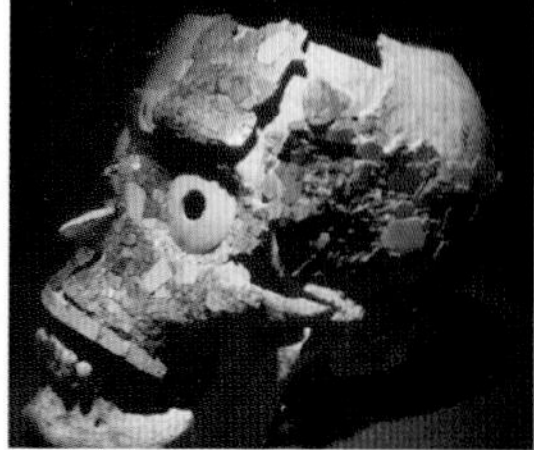

✉ Avenida Morelos 503 ☎ (951) 516 4750
🕒 Mon, Wed–Sat 10–2, 4–7, Sun 10–3
💰 Inexpensive

a walk around Oaxaca

This walk through the colonial heart of Oaxaca takes in churches, museums and the city's inimitable atmosphere.

Start at the zócalo *and head for the Catedral on the north side.*

Built in 1533, it contains a bronze altar, antique organ and, best of all, an elaborate 18th-century baroque facade.

Leave the Catedral, turning sharply right, and walk along Independencia to the pedestrian street of Alcalá. Turn left and walk uphill to the Museo de Arte Contemporáneo. After visiting, continue uphill, turn right along Murguia as far as Calle 5 de Mayo, then turn left. On your right is the Camino Real hotel (➤ 161).

This 400-year-old former convent, now a national monument, exudes a distinctive atmosphere.

Continue uphill to Santo Domingo (➤ 152) and visit both the church and adjacent museum (➤ 149). On leaving, turn right past the Instituto de Artes Gráficas to the Plazuela del Carmen Alto.

This small plaza is home to a colorful daily market of Oaxacan crafts.

Leave the plaza, turning left onto García Vigil. Continue downhill for four blocks before turning right into Morelos. Two blocks further is the Museo Rufino Tamayo (► 149). After visiting, continue another two blocks.

On the left is the 17th-century Basílica de la Soledad, home to a statue of the town's patron saint and a small museum.

Walk down the steps to Independencia. Turn left and walk four blocks east to the church of San Felipe Neri.

This church (1636) is noted for its fine frescoed walls and ornately gilded altar and nave.

Continue along Independencia to the zócalo.

Distance 2km (1 mile)
Time 3 hours including stops
Start/end point *Zócalo*
Lunch Café del Instituto de Artes Gráficas ($), Alcalá 507
? Check www.travel.state.gov.com or www.fco.gov.uk for the latest on safety in Oaxaca

Templo de Santo Domingo

Started in the late 16th century, this is one of Mexico's finest examples of baroque architecture. Above the main entrance is an extraordinary bas-relief genealogical tree of the family of Domingo de Guzmán, the 13th-century founder of the Dominican order. Beyond this, the soaring ceiling is entirely faced in elaborately gilded and painted stucco, surrounding 36 inset paintings. To the right is the Capilla del Rosario, another magnificent interpretation of Mexican baroque by indigenous artisans.

Alcalá, corner Gurrión · Mon–Sat 8–7:30, Sun 7–11, 1–7:30 · Free

The South

HUATULCO

Best places to see, ➤ 42–43.

MAZUNTE

This delightful, low-key fishing village lies 62km (39 miles) west of Huatulco, between Puerto Angel and Puerto Escondido. A beautiful adjoining beach, San Agustinillo, is popular with Mexicans for long lunches under shady *palapas*. Outlying rocks shelter the beach, making it ideal for those in search of calm waters and fresh seafood. Mazunte itself is home to the world's only turtle research center and the **Museo de la Tortuga,** an impressive modern set-up with turtles representing nine of the world's eleven types. The wild 15km (9-mile) beach north of here, not accessible by road, sees the arrival of some 200,000 Olive Ridley turtles during their nesting season, from July to December. Mazunte is also home to a local enterprise making natural cosmetics.

18M

Museo de la Tortuga

On main road (Mex 200) (958) 584 3055 Wed–Sat 10–4:30 Inexpensive Excellent seafood restaurants ($) in Playa San Agustinillo

MITLA

Meaning "place of the dead," this fascinating Zapotec site was occupied between AD400 and 700 but then became solely a ceremonial center. Much of the rich stone-carving was finished by the later Mixtecs, who alternated with the Zapotecs in regional power until the Spanish arrived in 1521. The structures are famed for their complex geometrical stonework, made using an inlay technique. This is particularly well preserved in the Grupo de las Columnas, which contains the masterful Patio de las Grecas. Nearby, another patio structure incorporates two underground cruciform tombs.

The remains of Mixtec murals are displayed in the grounds of the red-domed 16th-century church that rises above the site. Behind it is a large crafts market. The village is dominated by small crafts shops and *mezcal* bars, but don't miss the Frissell Museum, on the plaza at the entrance.

19L Highway 190, 45km (28 miles) southeast of Oaxaca Daily 8–5 Inexpensive; free Sun

MONTE ALBÁN

Best places to see, ➤ 44–45.

PALENQUE

Best places to see, ➤ 48–49.

PUERTO ANGEL

This charming fishing port, nestling between forested hills, has long been a favorite of those in the know, although many people just pass through en route for the halcyon charms of nearby Zipolite (➤ opposite) or sleepy Mazunte (➤ 153).

There is little to do here except laze on pretty Playa Panteon and watching diving pelicans, but the slow pace is appealing. Ultra-fresh seafood is provided by fishermen, who beach their boats or moor at the jetty. A short distance northwest is the hippie beach of Zipolite, where white sands ending in rocky headlands attract backpackers, while surfers revel in the often wild waves. Currents are dangerous and drownings have occurred.

18M 83km (52 miles) southeast of Puerto Escondido Restaurant Susy ($), Playa Panteon

PUERTO ESCONDIDO

Of the three beach resorts scattered along the Oaxacan coast, Puerto Escondido takes the middle road between sophisticated Huatulco (► 42–43) and relaxed Puerto Angel (► above). Its fishing-village past has receded somewhat with the influx of hotels, restaurants and shops, but the lovely curved bay is only the beginning; to the east lie palm-fringed Playa Marinero and the surfers' paradise of Playa Zicatela, while to the west is the pretty cove of Puerto Angelito, accessible by boat or road. From Playa Principal a walkway winds around the cliffs, offering sweeping sea views. Nightlife thrives in the form of low-key beach bars.

18L 264km (164 miles) south of Oaxaca

Boulevard Benito Juárez s/n, Fraccionamento Bacocho; tel: (954) 582 0175

SAN CRISTÓBAL DE LAS CASAS

This beautiful but once politically troubled town, high in the forested hills east of Tuxtla, remains a prime tourist favorite. Wood smoke fills the air in the narrow cobbled streets, shops offer an amazing array of local crafts, and hotels and restaurants are reasonable. Since the Zapatistas' uprising of 1994 and their protests of inequality being heard by the international community in 2005, things have vastly improved in rural areas. The town and surrounding countryside are consequently safer places to visit.

The main sights in town are the restored cathedral on the main square and, uphill on Avenida General Utrilla, the church of Santo Domingo (1547). Transformed in the 18th century, it presents a lacy, carved facade and an ornate baroque interior. Its terraces throng with a daily crafts market, while the adjoining monastery houses the **Centro Cultural de los Altos** and the weavers' co-operative, **Sna Jolobil**, which displays and sells examples of the skilled techniques still practised by local communities. Handicrafts continue two blocks north at the Mercado. East of here is Na-Bolom, an institution founded by Frans Blom and his wife Trudy, who researched and supported local communities, leaving this house as a legacy to anthropologists and writers, who stay here.

San Cristóbal is also the starting point for excursions to local villages. San Juan Chamula, 9km (6 miles) north, has a large Sunday market in front of its church. Here the Tzotzils combine elements of Christianity with ancient Mayan spiritual practices. Entry to the church is not allowed during religious ceremonies.

21L Delegacion de Turismo, Avenida Miguel Hidalgo 2; tel: (967) 678 6570/678 1467

Centro Cultural de los Altos

Ex-Convento de Santo Domingo (967) 81609 Daily 10–5
Inexpensive; free Sun

Sna Jolobil

Ex-Convento de Santo Domingo (967) 678 2646 Mon–Sat 9–2, 4–6
Free

TUXTLA GUTIÉRREZ

Although not an essential attraction in itself, Tuxtla is at the crossroads of several outstanding southern destinations. This modern capital of the state of Chiapas lies in a hot saucer rimmed by hills that rise in the east to San Cristóbal de las Casas. In the town center is the Parque Madero, a cultural complex containing a theater, botanic gardens, and the **Museo Regional,** which has a good display of Olmec and Mayan artifacts. To the south is a unique and enlightened zoo (➤ 71).

Chiapa de Corzo, 17km (10 miles) east on Highway 190, is the state's first Spanish settlement, dating from 1528. The arcaded main square encloses a fountain structure, La Pila, built to resemble the Spanish crown. One block away is the vast church of Santo Domingo, whose former convent houses the Museo de la Laca (lacquer museum), a local craft specialty. Just behind flows the Río Grijalva. From the *embarcadero* (jetty) boats leave for tours of the Cañon de Sumidero. This canyon, with depths of over 1,000m (3,280ft), can also be viewed from lookout points along a road north of Tuxtla.

20L

Belisario Domínguez 950; tel: (961) 602 5298

Museo Regional

Parque Madero (961) 613 4479 Tue–Sun 9–4 Inexpensive; free Sun

VERACRUZ

Known above all for its riotous Shrovetide carnival, Veracruz was also the place where Hernán Cortés and his men first landed in 1519. This major port on the Gulf of Mexico later witnessed the arrival of French forces in 1838, and in 1847 was bombarded by the Americans. As a result, many of its monuments date from the late 19th century, with the exception of the beautiful **Fortaleza de San Juan de Ulua,** built in the 16th century and later much extended. Lying north of town in the main port area, the fort's sturdy walls and bastions, which once enclosed a political prison and presidential palace, now contain a museum.

Life in central Veracruz revolves around the Plaza de Armas, flanked by the Catedral (1734) and the fine Palacio Municipal (1627), where hawkers vie with *marimba* bands long into the steamy night. The aquarium is also exceptional, but for swimming head south to the popular, though dirty, Mocambo beach, near Boca del Río.

19J

Fortaleza de San Juan de Ulua

Islote de San Juan de Ulúa (228) 938 5151 Tue–Sun 9–5 Drinks available Expensive

VILLAHERMOSA

The modern, oil-rich city of Villahermosa is famed, above all, for its relics of the sophisticated Olmec civilization, Mesoamerica's oldest. A large leisure complex, the Centro de Investigaciones de las Culturas Olmecas (CICOM), includes exceptional Olmec pieces at its Museo de Antropología, but it is at the **Parque Nacional de La Venta** that you will see the impressive giant heads that were hauled here from their original site at La Venta, 95km (59 miles) away. These now sit in a lush, wooded area that also houses an excellent zoo of local Tabasco animals. More insights into local nature lie at Yumka, a well-organized 100ha (247-acre) jungle, savannah and lagoon refuge for many endangered species (➤ 71).

21K

Avenue Los Rios y Calle 13, Tabasio 2000; tel: (993) 316 3633/ 316 2889

Parque Nacional de La Venta

Boulevard Adolfo Ruiz Cortines (933) 314 1652 Tue–Sat 9–4:30 Inexpensive; free Sun Cafeteria ($)

HOTELS

HUATULCO

Crown Pacific Huatulco ($$$)

The lavish hotel is built on a terraced hill overlooking Tangolunda Bay. There are lots of steps; some rooms are reached by funicular.

Boulevard Benito Juárez 8, Bahía Tangolunda (958) 581 0044; www.crownpacifichuatulco.com

OAXACA

Camino Real Oaxaca ($$$)

This stunning 16th-century convent has been converted into a luxury hotel with colonnaded cloisters and a fountained courtyard. It is a stunning example of Spanish baroque architecture. Rooms are airy, with high ceilings, bright decor and modern amenities.

5 de Mayo 300 (951) 501 6100; www.camino-real-oaxaca.com

Casa Oaxaca ($$$)

This superb, eclectic hotel is decorated with exceptional contemporary art indigenous to Oaxaca. There are seven spacious rooms, patios and a swimming pool. Breakfast is included in the very reasonable rates. No children under 12 years old.

García Vigil 407 (951) 514 4173; www.casaoaxaca.com.mx

PALENQUE

Chan-Kah Resort Village ($$$)

The beautifully sited *casitas* (bungalows) stand in lush jungle grounds very close to the archaeological ruins. There is a good restaurant and *cenote*-type pool.

Carretera a las Ruinas, Km 3 (916) 345 1100; www.chan-kah.com.mx

SAN CRISTÓBAL DE LAS CASAS

Holiday Inn San Cristóbal Español ($$)

The well-appointed rooms at this elegant, colonial-style hotel lead off from an attractive flowery patio. Facilities include a restaurant, bar, gym and solarium. Literary giants Ian Fleming and Graham Greene both stayed here.

Calle 1 de Marzo 15 (967) 678 0045; www.holidayinn.com

VERACRUZ

Fiesta Americana Veracruz ($$$)

This beachside hotel is popular with businesspeople and families. The large airy rooms have luxurious bathrooms. The hotel organizes children's activities and there are two restaurants.

Boulevard Avila Camacho (229) 989 8989; www.fiestamericana.com

VILLAHERMOSA

Best Western Hotel Maya Tabasco ($$–$$$)

Rooms at this small-scale hotel, close to La Venta Park and Villahermosa's museums, are comfortable and air-conditioned. Facilities include a pool, gym and restaurant.

Boulevard Adolfo Ruiz Cortinez 907 (993) 358 1111; www.hotelmaya.com.mx

RESTAURANTS

OAXACA

El Asador Vasco ($$)

Enjoy out-of-this-world Mexican cuisine, as well as Basque and international dishes at this central restaurant, close to the city's lively *zócalo*. Reservations are advised.

Portal de Flores (951) 514 4755; www.asadorvasco.com Daily 1:30–11:30

La Casa de la Abuela ($$)

Head to this quaint hideaway to sample some classic Oaxacan cuisine, served with a variety of *mole* sauces and crumbly white Oaxacan cheese. Reservations are suggested.

Avenida Hidalgo 616, Altos (951) 516 3544 Daily 1–10

Casa Oaxaca ($$$)

➤ 58.

La Catrina de Alcalá ($$)

On Oaxaca's popular pedestrian walkway, this welcoming restaurant is one of the best places in the city to see and be seen. Dine on beautifully presented Oaxacan fare to the tune of a hidden troubadour and water cascading from the centrepiece stone fountain. The restaurant shares space with a boutique hotel and art gallery, giving it a bohemian feel.

✉ Macedonio Alcalá 102 ☎ (951) 514 5704; www.restaurantelacatrina.com

💎💎 Mezzaluna Ristorante ($)

Celebrated for its thin-crust pizzas cooked in a wood-fired oven, and for its antipasti, soups, salads and deserts, Mezzaluna is housed in an old mansion brimming with atmosphere.

✉ Ignacio Allende 113, Centro ☎ (951) 516 8195 🕐 Daily 1–11

SAN CRISTÓBAL DE LAS CASAS

💎💎 Restaurante Plaza Real ($)

Housed in a former government building and shaded by ficus trees, this well-presented restaurant turns out pasta, salads, vegetarian, international and Mexican cuisine.

✉ Real de Guadalupe 55 ☎ (967) 678 0992 🕐 Daily 7am–11pm

SHOPPING

ART AND ANTIQUES

Galería Gráfica Soruco

A wide selection of etchings, lithographs, engravings and oils, all created by celebrated local artists, are for sale at this gallery in Oaxaca.

✉ Plazuela Labastida 104C, Oaxaca ☎ (951) 514 3938

Galerías Huatulco

The gallery sells contemporary paintings and sculptures by artists from Oaxaca, Morelos, Michoacán and Jalisco, as well as interesting jewelry designs in gold and silver.

✉ Hotel Sheraton, Bahía Tangolunda, Huatulco ☎ (958) 581 0080

🕐 Mon–Sat 9–1, 5–7, Sun 9–2

Galería Quetzalli

See works by some of the best young Oaxacan artists at this large contemporary art gallery. Combined with a bar-restaurant.

✉ Constitución 104, Oaxaca ☎ (951) 514 2606 🕐 Mon–Sat 10–2, 5–8

La Mano Mágica

This long-established Oaxacan art gallery hosts regular exhibitions of contemporary artists. Handicrafts are sold in an adjacent store.

✉ Alcalá 203, Oaxaca ☎ (951) 516 4275 🕐 Mon–Sat 10:30–3, 4:30–8

CLOTHES AND ACCESSORIES

Dishvé

If you want a change from Oaxaca's indigenous embroidered clothes, the cheesecloth and cotton women's wear and range of accessories at Dishvé may be the answer. See next door, too.

✉ Plaza Santo Domingo, Alcalá 407, Oaxaca ☎ (951) 514 2913

HANDICRAFTS

Casa de las Artesanías de Oaxaca

Selling the collected works of 80 different families, this shop is a treasure trove of authentic local handicrafts, including beautiful rugs and ceramics.

✉ Matamoros 105, Oaxaca

Instituto Oaxaqueno de las Artesanías

This government-run artists's cooperative sells work from around the state. The selection of painted copal-wood animals is particularly fine.

✉ Calle García Vigil 809, Oaxaca ☎ (951) 514 2101

Mujeres Artesanas de las Regiones de Oaxaca

Craftswork by a local women's cooperative is on display in this sprawling showroom/store. Take your pick from the wonderful collection of pottery, woodcarvings, weaving, embroidered clothes, leatherwork and much more. Shipping can be arranged.

✉ Calle 5 de Mayo 204, Oaxaca ☎ (951) 516 0670

JEWELRY

Jade Artesanías

This shop sells Oaxacan handicrafts alongside replica jewelry and objects.

✉ García Vigil 703, Oaxaca ☎ (951) 516 0519

Oro de Monte Albán

The fabulous array of gold reproductions of the Mixtec jewelry discovered at Monte Albán is not to be missed. This is one of several outlets.

✉ Alcalá 403, Oaxaca ☎ (951) 514 3813

MARKETS

Mercado de Artesanías

At this large crafts market southwest of Oaxaca's *zócalo*, you'll find rugs, textiles, jewelry, painted wooden animals and ceramics for sale. Bargaining is essential.

✉ Zaragoza, corner J P García, Oaxaca 🕑 Daily 11–8

Mercado José Castillo Tielmans

The daily market in San Cristóbal de las Casas serves as the main indigenous market for surrounding villages. There is a fabulous array of crafts, with great ethnic diversity.

✉ Avenida General Utrilla, corner Nicaragua, San Cristóbal de las Casas
🕑 Mon–Sat 6–3

ENTERTAINMENT

Magic Circus Disco Club

Attached to Hotel Marlin at western end of Santa Cruz, this club plays mainly international rock on its domed dance floor. Live bands also play here.

✉ Andador Huatulco 102, Santa Cruz, Huatulco ☎ (958) 587 0017
🕑 Thu–Sat nights

Mágico Trópico

Enjoy live tropical and Latino music – *salsa* and more.

✉ Gardenia 311 Altos, opposite Hotel Flamboyant, Huatulco ☎ (958) 587 0702

Poison

Party the night away at this hip, partly open-air nightclub up a dirt road behind Huatulco's marina.

✉ Bahía de Santa Cruz, Huatulco ☎ (958) 587 1530

Yumka

➤ 71.

SPORTS AND ACTIVITIES

Centro de Buceo Curazao

This Veracruz dive shop also rents out diving gear and organizes diving trips. It handles windsurfing and sport fishing, too.

✉ Boca del Río, Veracruz ☎ (228) 822 2033

Community Museums of Oaxaca

A union of 16 Oaxacan villages provide tours of the region, giving a unique insight into their culture and way of life. They are specialists in all types of eco-tours, including walking, horseback riding and bicycle trips.

✉ Constitució, Oaxaca ☎ (951) 516 2991; www.oaxaca.com/museums.htm

Eco-Discover Tours

Eco-Discover Tours arranges adventure trips round Huatulco's bays, specializing in mountain biking and scuba diving, although horseback riding, kayaking and hiking can also be arranged.

✉ Plaza Las Conchas L-6, Bahía Tangolunda, Huatulco ☎ (958) 581 0002

Iguana Expediciones

This company offers a range of caving, rappelling, mountain biking, rafting, kayaking and scuba diving in the Veracruz area.

✉ Cotaxtla Sur 16, Colonia Petrolera, Boca del Río, Veracruz ☎ (228) 821 1550

Jungle Tour

This Huatulco-based operator runs quad bike (ATV) tours of the jungle around the reserves of Maguey and Organo Bays, with lunch on a beach.

✉ Lobby of Hotel Royal Maeva, Bahía Tangolunda, Huatulco ☎ (958) 581 0000

Saddling South

➤ 60.

Mérida and the Yucatán Peninsula

Jutting out between the Gulf of Mexico and the Caribbean is a flat limestone shelf riddled with underground rivers, caves and *cenotes* (sinkholes). Above ground this peninsula is less than inspiring, consisting mainly of monotonous savannah and low jungle. Yet it continues to attract charter-loads of visitors.

The reason is quite simple; this was the heartland of the great Maya culture and, along with Guatemala, claims their most astonishing monuments. Chichén Itzá, Uxmal, Cobá and Tulúm, as well as many lesser-known sites, are a magnet for the historically inclined visitor. And beyond them lie the aquamarine depths of the Caribbean, where underwater life is hard to surpass. Lining the coast is a string of resorts, starting with Cancún, that cater to every touristic and hedonistic whim.

MÉRIDA

The elegant capital of the state of Yucatán makes a relaxed base for exploring major Mayan ruins such as Chichén Itzá (➤ 38–39) and Uxmal (➤ 180). Mérida has a strong sense of history and culture, much of which has been absorbed from its links with the US, Cuba, Europe and even the Middle East. This unusually cosmopolitan flavor expanded further in the 1950s when direct road and rail links were established with Mexico City.

When the Spaniards arrived in 1542, led by Francisco de Montejo, they used the stones of the declining Mayan city of T'ho to erect their cathedral and administrative structures. But it was not until the late 19th century that Mérida's fortunes really changed. The catalyst was the burgeoning sisal industry, whose prosperous French investors bequeathed an impressive *belle époque* architectural style. Today, many of the earlier colonial buildings around the *zócalo* have been restored, while to the north the tree-lined Paseo de Montejo is home to a string of grandiose edifices that were the residences of the sisal-empire builders. This area is now regarded as "modern" Mérida, characterized by airline offices, large hotels and nightclubs.

South of the *zócalo*, in the streets surrounding the sprawling market, is a more mundane but authentic quarter, where everywhere you will see diminutive Mayan women in embroidered white dresses and older gentlemen in their immaculate white *guayaberas* (tucked shirts).

22H

Calle 59 No 514; tel: (999) 930 3760

Casa de Montejo

This is Mérida's first Spanish house, built in 1549 by the conquistador Francisco de Montejo. His descendants lived there until only a few years ago, but today the mansion more prosaically houses a branch of Banamex (bank). The facade is an outstanding example of the Plateresque style, with sculpted busts and the Montejo coat of arms depicting two soldiers triumphing over the bodies of prostrate Maya.

Plaza Mayor, Calle 63

Mon–Fri 9–5 Free

Cafés and restaurants ($–$$) on square

Catedral de San Ildefonso

Built between 1556 and 1599, this is said to be the oldest cathedral on the American continent, although Campeche's inhabitants would not agree. The massive edifice was built with the stones of the dismantled Mayan town of T'ho, but during the 1915 Revolution it was stripped bare. Today's worshipers venerate an impressive 7m (23ft) statue of Christ that dominates the lofty stone interior. Other sights flanking the main square outside are the Palacio Municipal (1735) opposite, and the Palacio de Gobierno (1892) on the northern side, whose interior displays a remarkable series of 27 paintings depicting the complex history of the Maya, Spaniards and Mexicans.

✉ Plaza Mayor, Calle 60 🕒 Daily 6am–7pm ✋ Free 🍴 Cafés and restaurants ($–$$) on square and along Calle 60

Museo de Antropología e Historia

On Mérida's most luxurious avenue, this elaborate 1911 mansion was built for the state governor to rival others belonging to prosperous sisal barons. As a result, the interior Doric columns, marble, chandeliers and extravagant mouldings somewhat overpower the exhibits. These offer a clear background to the history of the Yucatán, its Mayan sites and culture. Artifacts include a rare collection of jade offerings recovered from the *cenote* at Chichén Itzá.

✉ Palacio Canton, Paseo de Montejo 485 ☎ (999) 923 0557 🕒 Tue–Sat 8–8, Sun 8–2 ✋ Moderate; free Sun 🍴 Cafés and restaurants ($–$$) along Paseo de Montejo

The Yucatán Peninsula

CAMPECHE

Founded in the 1540s, Campeche suffered repeated attacks from pirates, and it was not until the erection of thick walls and eight bastions in the late 17th century that it prospered. There are two excellent museums and several interesting churches, including the Catedral on the main square and the 16th-century church of San Francisco. In the central Baluarte de la Soledad is a superb display of Mayan stelae (carved stone slabs). A **museum** in the hilltop Fuerte de San Miguel has a rare collection of Maya jade and pottery.

22J

Avenida Ruiz Cortines s/n, Plaza Moch-Couoh; tel: (981) 811 9255

Museo Histórico Fuerte de San Miguel

4km (2.5 miles) south of Campeche Tue–Sun 9–8, Sun 9–1

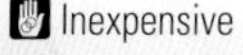
Inexpensive

CANCÚN

Situated on a peninsula of land that was uninhabited until the 1970s, Mexico's premier resort draws some 4 million visitors every year. Many come from the US and Europe to visit its beautiful beaches and to sample its hedonistic atmosphere. This is hardly the "real" Mexico, but makes an easy base for heading inland or further south along the increasingly developed "Maya Riviera." Most visitors come on package holidays and their 24-hour needs are well catered to. Long before the tourists came there was a small Mayan settlement here. Its remains are visible at the Ruinas del Rey and at the **Museo Arqueológico.**

24H

Centro de Convenciones, Boulevard Kukulcán, Km 9; tel: (998) 884 6531

Museo Arqueológico

Centro de Convenciones, Boulevard Kukulcán, Km 9 (998) 883 6671

Tue–Sun 8–7 Moderate; free Sun

CHICHÉN ITZÁ

Best places to see, ➤ 38–39.

COBÁ

This lakeside Mayan site remains little visited, despite its significance in the web of *sacbeob* (sacred "white paths") connecting other historic sites. Only a tiny proportion of this enormous city has been excavated, and these ruins are scattered through the jungle, so bring sturdy shoes, water and insect repellent. Immediately visible is the Grupo de Cobá, whose narrow, steep pyramid rises over 30m (98ft) above the tree-tops to give sweeping views over the lake. A ball court is next on the trail, followed by the Conjunto de las Pinturas (Temple of the Painted Ladies), some carved stelae and altars known as the Grupo Macanxoc. Nearly 3km (2 miles) further on towers 42m-high (138ft) Nohoch Mul, the tallest pyramid in the northern Yucatán peninsula. A strenuous climb is rewarded by a small temple decorated with descending god figures.

24H · 42km (26 miles) northwest of Tulúm · (98) 324634 · Daily 7am–6pm · Moderate; free Sun · Cafés and restaurants ($)

a drive from Cancún to Cobá

This drive takes you inland from Cancún to the colonial town of Valladolid and the Mayan site of Cobá. A dip in a *cenote* is an option.

Drive west out of Cancún along Avenida López Portillo following signs for Valladolid/Mérida. Avoid the cuota *highway (a pricey tollroad, though quicker) and remain on the old Highway 180 which takes you through a string of pretty rural villages.*

Traditional Mayan houses are generally elliptical in shape with tightly aligned tree-branch walls and *palapa* (thatched palm-leaf) roofs.

Drive 159km (99 miles) to Valladolid, watching out for the countless topes *(speed bumps) that pepper every village. Drive straight into Valladolid's main plaza then follow Calle 41 west for two blocks, where it forks. Go left (Calle 41a) for another three blocks.*

In front of you stands the bright yellow San Bernardino de Siena, a 16th-century Franciscan church and monastery. Often targeted by indigenous rebellions, the interior is practically bare.

Continue southwest a few blocks to the Cenote Dzitnup, signposted on the outskirts.

Have a refreshing dip in this beautiful *cenote* before returning to the main plaza. Park, visit the church of San Servacio, shop, then have lunch.

*Drive back 28km (17 miles) along Highway 180 to Chemax and turn right to Cobá. Another 30km (19 miles) brings you to this archaeological site (**➤ 173**). Leave Cobá by following signs to Tulúm, then watch for a turn-off to the left after a few kilometers/miles. This brings you to Tres Reyes and back to Highway 180 or the toll road to Cancún.*

Distance 350km (217 miles)
Time 9–10 hours (including stops)
Start/end point Avenida López Portillo, Cancún ✚ 24H
Lunch Hotel María de la Luz ($), Plaza Principal, Valladolid; tel: (985) 856 2071

COZUMEL

Like Cancún, the island of Cozumel is almost entirely geared to the needs of tourists. Cruise ship passengers, scuba divers and Cancunites all come to taste the delights of the renowned Palankar Reef, one of the world's top diving destinations. Unfortunately the most visited beach, Chankanab, now offers mainly dead coral, although the fish are spectacular. Skilled divers make day trips to some 20 different sites further out. Good swimming beaches dot the southwestern corner of the island, but strong currents make the eastern coast dangerous. In the unspoiled north lies a late Mayan site, **San Gervasio,** with a temple dedicated to Ixchel, goddess of fertility. The main town, San Miguel, is a modernized place, where, again, the flavor of real Mexico is virtually absent.

24H

Plaza del Sol, in the *zócalo*; tel: (987) 869 0211

San Gervasio

13km (8 miles) northeast of San Miguel; tel: (987) 800 2215 Daily 7–5

Frequent ferries from Playa del Carmen, boat trips from Cancún

GRUTAS DE LOLTÚN

These spectacular underground caves and galleries lie in the heart of the undulating Puuc Hills, south of Mérida. Inhabited over 2,500 years ago, their secret network was also used by rebellious Maya seeking refuge during the mid-19th-century Caste War. Fabulous rock formations, cave paintings, musical stalactites and the Cathedral, a large chamber that soars over 50m (164ft) high, are all part of this compelling underworld.

23J 115km (71 miles) south of Mérida, 50km (31 miles) east of Uxmal Daily guided tours at 9:30, 11, 12:30, 2, 3:30 Moderate

Café ($) at entrance

ISLA MUJERES

This delightful little island has a sleepy rhythm of its own. Most streets are of sand, cars are outnumbered by golf-carts and bicycles, and nights are tranquil. It makes an enticing escape from the over-development on Cancún, and as well as good beaches and diving, offers several attractions. The main town and services adjoin Playa Norte, while at the far southern tip is **El Garrafón,** a national park covering part of the Great Mayan Reef. Although the coral is dead, boat trips take snorkelers and divers to better spots farther afield.

Half-way down the central lagoon lies Dolphin Discovery, a registered dolphin center, near a turtle farm. A small altar to the fertility goddess Ixchel explains the island's name ("Island of Women"); when the Spanish first landed they found numerous statues of her. Day trips also go to the Isla Contoy bird sanctuary.

24H

Rueda Medina, opposite jetty; tel: (998) 877 0307

Parque Nacional El Garrafón

Carretera al Faro (998) 877 1100 Daily 8:30–6:30 Expensive Snack bar ($) on terrace

PLAYA DEL CARMEN

Once a beach-bum's paradise, this small resort is mushrooming fast. The modern town center is built on a narrow grid of streets bisected by Avenida 5, a favorite promenading and restaurant strip, ending at palm-fringed Caribbean beaches. South of the Cozumel ferry pier is an airstrip and golf course, while north of town hotels are rapidly eating up the shore. Nightlife, eating and shopping opportunities are plentiful, but there is little else.

24H Free info-line 1-800-GO-PLAYA

TULÚM

This dramatically situated Mayan ruin (AD900–1500) rises perilously on a cliff edge north of a slowly expanding stretch of hotels. Inland lies a typical services town without much beauty but with reasonable prices. However, if you want a few quiet days of sleeping beside the waves, Tulum's beach accommodation is ideal.

The ruins themselves are now fronted by a large shopping plaza from where a tram ferries visitors to the site, although it is within easy walking distance. Sadly, this structure has taken away much of Tulúm's drama, but the Templo de los Frescos is still remarkable for its faded interior murals, the palace for its carved figures, and the Castillo complex for its serpentine columns and sweeping sea views.

24J Highway 307 Daily 8–5 Moderate; free Sun Snack bars ($) in plaza

UXMAL

Uxmal was founded between the fifth and sixth centuries AD and at one point had some 25,000 inhabitants, before being abandoned around 900. It stands on a wide plateau in the Puuc Hills, near several smaller sites of similar style. Outstanding is the Pirámide del Adivino (Magician's Pyramid), an elliptical structure rising over 40m (130ft). Immediately to the west stands the Cuadrángulo de las Monjas (The Nuns' Quadrangle), where fine stone inlay typifies the Puuc style. South of here is an elevated complex, the Palacio del Gobernador (Governor's Palace) showing unsurpassed decorative techniques. Beyond is the Casa de las Tortugas (House of the Turtles), the Gran Pirámide (Great Pyramid), and the Casa de la Vieja (Old Lady's House). Visitors with guides can see the last two structures, where numerous sculpted phalluses at the Templo de los Falos (Temple of Phalluses) point to a unique cult in Uxmal.

22J · 78km (48 miles) south of Mérida on Highway 261 · Daily 8–5
Restaurant ($) in museum complex · Expensive; moderate Sun
Spectacular sound-and-light show at 7pm in Spanish, 9pm in English

HOTELS

CANCÚN

Hilton Cancun Beach and Golf Resort ($$$)

Dramatic pyramid building with extensive pool areas and the largest beach area of any hotel in Cancún. All rooms have views of the Caribbean. Facilities include an 18-hole golf course and excellent spa center.

Boulevard Kukulcán, Km 17 (998) 881 8000; www1.hilton.com

Hotel Riu Caribe

This beachside behemoth has an all inclusive system favored by families. Facilities include a swimming pool, a 200m (218-yard) beach, tennis courts, volleyball and water-sports center.

Boulevard Kukulcán, Km 5.5, Lote 6-C (998) 848 7850; www.riu.com

CHICHÉN ITZÁ

Hacienda Chichén Resort ($$$)

Enjoy modern air-conditioned cottage accommodation at this lovely 16th-century hacienda hotel. Facilities include the beautiful gardens, swimming pool and restaurant.

Chichén Itzá (985) 851 0045; www.haciendachichen.com

COZUMEL

Playa Azul Hotel ($$$)

This small-scale, environmentally friendly hotel lies toward the northern end of the island. Rooms overlook a secluded beach or gardens. Azul also offers guests complimentary golf at the nearby Cozumel Country Club (course designed by the Nicklaus Group).

Carretera San Juan, Km 4 (987) 872 0199; www.playa-azul.com

ISLA MUJERES

Hotel Secreto ($$$)

Super-chic Secreto sits on the quietest part of the northern tip of Isla Mujeres, and with its minimal style and beautiful lap pool, it is the perfect place to unwind. Rooms have huge beds, WiFi, plasma TV screens and pleasing contemporary furniture.

Secc Roca, Lote 11 (998) 877 1039; www.hotelsecreto.com

MÉRIDA

Hotel Casa del Balam ($$$)

A stylish central hotel, Casa del Balam occupies a modernized 19th-century building. Facilities include soundproofing, swimming pool, colonial features, satellite TV, travel agency and parking.

Calle 60 No 488 (999) 924 8844; www.casadelbalam.com

Hotel Julamis ($$)

An intimate boutique hotel with seven beautiful rooms based around a peaceful hacienda courtyard, Julamis fuses the traditional elements of its old villa with contemporary Mexican and Lebanese touches. The staff are welcoming and courteous.

Calle 53 455B por Calle 54 (999) 924 1818; www.hoteljulamis.com

PLAYA DEL CARMEN

Mandarin Oriental Riviera Maya ($$$)

This huge 128 room hotel stands right by the waves, with bungalow-style villas spread about its jungle-themed gardens. There is an excellent spa, a gym and a number of restaurants.

Carretera Federal Km 298.8 (984) 877 3888; www.mandarinoriental.com

UXMAL

The Lodge at Uxmal ($$$)

The Lodge at Uxmal offers a blend of Mayan and European architectural styles, two pools, plus views of Uxmal. The restaurant serves Mexican, Yucatecan and international cuisine.

At the main entrance to the archaeological site (987) 976 2031

RESTAURANTS

CANCÚN

Captain's Cove ($$)

A favorite for some 20 years, this fine restaurant excels with delicious food and a superb lagoon-facing location. Mouthwatering dishes fresh from the ocean include lobster and calamari (squid), plus the catch of the day cooked on the open grill.

Boulevard Kukulcán, Km 9.5 (998) 885 0016; www.captainscoverestaurant.com Daily 2–11pm

La Dolce Vita ($$$)

Enjoy excellent Italian cuisine and attentive service at this established restaurant. Choose from the delicious fresh pasta, seafood or salads. Reservations are advisable.

Boulevard Kukulcán, Km 14.6, opposite Hotel Marriott (998) 885 0161; www.cancunitalianrestaurant.com Lunch and dinner

COZUMEL

La Choza ($–$$)

This basic *cantina* serves up dishes such as red snapper enchiladas and chili *felanos* with warm service. Expect traditonal Yucatán cuisine delivered with flair.

Avenida 10 Sur (987) 872 0958; www.lachozacozumel.com
7:30am–10:30pm

ISLA MUJERES

Restaurant Zazil Ha

The *palapa*-style beachfront restaurant of the Na Balam hotel serves some of the best seafood on the island. Alternatively, try the chicken stuffed with corn, mushrooms and goat's cheese. There is a decent vegetarian menu, plus Mexican staples such as tacos, nachos and tasty fresh fruit juices.

Calle Zazil Ha 118 (998) 877 0279; www.nabalam.com/dining.htm
Daily 7:30am–10:30pm

MÉRIDA

Los Almendros ($$)

A fine choice of local specialties are served at this famous Yucatecan restaurant: black beans and pork, turkey broth with pickled onions, enchiladas and more. There's also a three-piece band to keep you entertained while you eat your meal. Reservations are advisable.

Calle 50-A No 493, Plaza de la Mejorada (999) 923 8135 Daily 9am–11pm

La Casona ($$)

➤ 58–59.

Portico del Peregrino $$$

Set in a lush courtyard in the heart of Mérida, this is a peaceful spot to savor locally sourced seafood and other typical Yucatán dishes. Come armed with a hearty appetite as portions here are generous.

Calle 57 501 por 60 y 62 (999) 928 6163 Daily 12–12

SHOPPING

CLOTHING AND ACCESSORIES

Karla and Maria Artisans Boutique

Take your pick from the beautiful clothing sourced from all over Mexico. The colorfully patterned dresses are a highlight.

Avenida Hidalgo, Central Isla Mujeres Mon–Sat 10–5

MARKET

Mercado Municipal de Artesanías

This sprawling crafts market sells embroidered dresses, lace, hammocks and Panama hats. Made-to-measure clothes are also available, though take a couple of days to complete.

Calle 65, corner Calle 56, behind post office, Mérida Daily 9–5

ENTERTAINMENT

Cancún Queen

Enjoy a paddle-steamer cruise through the mangroves of Nichupté Lagoon with three-course dinner, live band, dancing and games.

Aquaworld, Boulevard Kukulcán 15, Cancún (998) 885 5228 Daily at 6:30pm

Carlos n' Charlies

Something of a Cancún legend, this is the type of joint where the staff often join the band on stage and the conga line just grows.

Boulevard Kukulcán, Km 5.5, Cancún (998) 849 4053 Daily noon–5am

Coco Bongo

Mixing a carnival atmosphere of trapeze artists, conga lines and multimedia projected on its walls, Coco Bongo draws rave reviews for its eclectic range of music and explosions of confetti and foam onto its unsuspecting guests.

✉ Boulevard Kukulcán, Km 9.5, 30 Plaza Mall, Cancún ☎ (998) 883 5061 🕐 Daily 10:30pm–5am

Dady'O

This gigantic and legendary disco has tiered seating, blinding laser shows and mainly techno rhythms.

✉ Boulevard Kukulcán, Km 9.5, Cancún ☎ (998) 883 3333 🕐 Daily from 10pm

Mango Tango

Head to Mango's red-hot dance floor for salsa, tango and Latin dancing. Good Argentine meat and seafood dishes are served.

✉ Boulevard Kukulcán, Km 14.2, opposite Ritz-Carlton Hotel, Cancún ☎ (998) 885 0303 🕐 Dinner show starts at 8pm daily

SPORTS AND ACTIVITIES

Aquaworld

➤ 70.

Dolphin Discovery

➤ 70.

Diving Adventures

Scuba diving school, full PADI certificates. Daily boat dives for all levels. Nitrox dives available.

✉ Calle 5 No 2, San Miguel, Cozumel ☎ (987) 872 3009

Sea Hawk Divers

➤ 60.

Wet 'n Wild

➤ 71.

Xcaret

➤ 71.

Index

Is there anything we could have done better? ______________________________

____

____

____

About you...

Name (*Mr/Mrs/Ms*) ______________________________

Address ______________________________

____

______________________________ Postcode ____________

Daytime tel nos ______________________________

Email ______________________________

Please only give us your mobile phone number or email if you wish to hear from us about other products and services from the AA and partners by text or mms, or email.

Which age group are you in?

Under 25 ☐ 25–34 ☐ 35–44 ☐ 45–54 ☐ 55–64 ☐ 65+ ☐

How many trips do you make a year?

Less than one ☐ One ☐ Two ☐ Three or more ☐

Are

Ab

Wh

Ho

Wa

Di

If

T
p

AA Travel Insurance call

The information we hold about you will be used to provide the products and services requested and for identification, account administration, analysis, and fraud/loss prevention purposes. More details about how that information is used is in our privacy statement, which you'll find under the heading "Personal Information" in our terms and conditions and on our website: www.theAA.com. Copies are also available from us by post, by contacting the Data Protection Manager at AA, Fanum House, Basing View, Basingstoke, Hampshire RG21 4EA.

We may want to contact you about other products and services provided by us, or our partners (by mail, telephone or email) but please tick the box if you DO NOT wish to hear about such products and services from us by mail, telephone or email. ☐

Dear Reader

Your comments, opinions and recommendations are very important to us. Please help us to improve our travel guides by taking a few minutes to complete this simple questionnaire.

You do not need a stamp (unless posted outside the UK). If you do not want to cut this page from your guide, then photocopy it or write your answers on a plain sheet of paper.

Send to: **The Editor, AA World Travel Guides, FREEPOST SCE 4598, Basingstoke RG21 4GY.**

Your recommendations...

We always encourage readers' recommendations for restaurants, nightlife or shopping – if your recommendation is used in the next edition of the guide, we will send you a **FREE AA Guide** of your choice from this series. Please state below the establishment name, location and your reasons for recommending it.

____

____

____

____

____

____

Please send me **AA Guide** ____________________________

About this guide...

Which title did you buy?

AA ______________________________________

Where did you buy it? ______________________________

When? m m / y y

Why did you choose this guide? __________________________

____

____

____

____

Did this guide meet your expectations?

Exceeded ☐ Met all ☐ Met most ☐ Fell below ☐

Were there any aspects of this guide that you particularly liked? ______________

____

____

____

continued on next page...

Sight locator index

This index relates to the maps on the cover. We have given map references to the main sights in the book. Some sights may not be plotted on the maps.

Acknowledgements

The Automobile Association would like to thank the following photographers, companies and picture libraries for their assistance in the preparation of this book.

Abbreviations for the picture credits are as follows – (t) top; (b) bottom; (c) centre; (l) left; (r) right; (AA) AA World Travel Library.

4l Taxco, AA/R Strange; **4c** Teotihuacán, AA/R Strange; **4r** View from the Pyramid of the Moon across the site built by an ancient civilization Teotihuacán, AA/C Sawyer; **5l** Guadalupe, AA/R Strange; **5r** Guanajuato, AA/C Sawyer; **6/7** Taxco, AA/R Strange; **8/9** Horse, AA/C Sawyer; **10cl** Tiled building, AA/C Sawyer; **10/lt** traditional hat, AA/C Sawyer; **10/1c** Day of the Dead papier mache figure, AA/R Strange; **10br** Mariachi, AA/C Sawyer; **11tr** Puebla, AA/C Sawyer; **11tcr** Xilitla, AA/R Strange; **11bcr** Loreto, AA/L Dunmire; **11br** El Tajin, AA/R Strange; **12/3t** Street vendors, AA/C Sawyer; **12/3b** Food, AA/C Sawyer; **13t** Barmen, AA/C Sawyer; **14** Restaurant, AA/C Sawyer; **15bl** Tequila, AA/R Strange; **15tr** Fish Market, AA/R Strange; **15cr** Alcoholic drinks, AA/C Sawyer; **15br** Mezcal, AA/R Strange; **16** Cathedral, AA/C Sawyer; **16/7** Puerto Vallarta, AA/R Strange; **17t** Macaw, AA/R Strange; **17b** Lake Patzcuaro, AA/R Strange; **18** Scuba diving; AA/R Strange; **18/9** Market, AA/C Sawyer; **19tr** Flower Seller, AA/R Strange; **19br** Chichén Itzá, AA/R Strange; **19bl** Artefact, AA/R Strange; **20/1** Teotihuacan, AA/R Strange; **24/5** Pilgrims, AA/R Strange; **26** Cruise Liner, AA/L Dunmire; **27** Bus, AA/C Sawyer; **30** Telephone, AA/L Dunmire; **31** Sign, AA/R Strange; **32** Policeman, AA/C Sawyer; **34/5** View from the Pyramid of the Moon across the site built by an ancient civilization Teotihuacán, AA/C Sawyer; **36** Batopilas, AA/ F Dunlop; **36/7** Batopilas, AA/F Dunlop; **38/9t** Chichén Itzá, AA/R Strange; **38/9b** Chichén Itzá, AA/R Strange; **40** Guanajuato, AA/C Sawyer; **40/1** Guanajuato, AA/C Sawyer; **41t** Museo de las Momías, AA/R Strange; **42** Beach at Tangolunda in Huatulco, AA/C Sawyer; **42/3** Huatulco, AA/C Sawyer; **44/5** Monte Alban, AA/R Strange; **45** Monte Alban, AA/R Strange; **46/7** Museo Nacional de Antropología, AA/C Sawyer; **48** Palenque, AA/C Sawyer; **48/9** Palenque, AA/C Sawyer; **50/1** Taxco, AA/R Strange; **51** Taxco, AA/C Sawyer; **52** Teotihuacán, AA/C Sawyer; **52/3t** Teotihuacán, AA/R Strange; **52/3b** Teotihuacán, AA/R Strange; **54/5** Xochimilco, AA/R Strange; **56/7** Guadalupe, AA/R Strange; **59** Restaurant, AA/C Sawyer; **60/1** Golf, AA/C Sawyer; **62/3** Yagul, AA/S Watkins; **64/5** Puebla, AA/C Sawyer; **66/7** Queretaro, AA/C Sawyer; **68/9** Janitzio, AA/C Sawyer; **70/1** CICI, AA/C Sawyer; **71** Bosque de Chapultepec, AA/C Sawyer; **72/3** Hut and boats at Sian Ka'an Biosphere, AA/C Sawyer; **74/5** Loreto, AA/L Dunmire; **76/7** Guanajuato, AA/C Sawyer; **79** Children playing, AA/C Sawyer; **80** Palacio Nacional, AA/C Sawyer; **80/1** Bosque de Chapultepec, AA/C Sawyer; **82** Museo Anahuacalli, AA/R Strange; **82/3** Cathedral, AA/C Sawyer; **84** San Angel, AA/C Sawyer; **84/5** San Angel, AA/C Sawyer; **86/7** Museo Frida Kahlo, AA/C Sawyer; **87** Palacio de bellas Artes, AA/P Wilson; **88** Palacio Nacional, AA/C Sawyer; **88/9** Templo Mayor, AA/R Strange; **90** Cholula, AA/R Strange; **90/1** Mariachis, AA/C Sawyer; **92/3** Guadalajara, AA/R Strange; **94** Laguna de Chapala, AA/R Strange; **95** Patzcuaro, AA/C Sawyer; **96** Puebla, AA/C Sawyer; **97** Queretaro, AA/C Sawyer; **98** Patzcuaro, AA/C Sawyer; **98/9** Janitzio, AA/C Sawyer; **100/1** El Tajin; AA/R Strange; **101** Xalapa, AA/P Wilson; **113** Ensenada, AA/L Dunmire; **114** Chihuahua Pacifico railroad, AA/P Wilson; **114/5** Casas Grande, AA/P Wilson; **115** Chihuahua, AA/P Wilson; **116/7** Ensenda, AA/P Wilson; **117** Hermosillo, AA/P Wilson; **118/9** La Paz, AA/L Dunmire; **120** Los Cabos, AA/L Dunmire; **121** Todos Santos, AA/L Dunmire; **122/3t** Loreto, AA/L Dunmire; **122/3b** Loreto, AA/L Dunmire; **124/5** Museo de Mulege, AA/L Dunmire; **125** San Ignacio, AA/L Dunmire; **131** Puerto Vallarta, AA/P Wilson; **132** Acapulco, AA/C Sawyer; **132/3** CICI, AA/C Sawyer; **133** Acapulco, AA/C Sawyer; **134/5** La Quebrada, AA/R Strange; **135** View to Isla Ixtapa, AA/ R Strange; **136/7** Puerto Vallarta, AA/R Strange; **138** Puerto Vallarta, AA/R Strange; **139** Puerto Vallarta, AA/R Strange; **147** Local people, AA/C Sawyer; **148** Oaxaca, AA/R Strange; **148/9** Oaxaca, AA/R Strange; **149** Rufino Tamayo Museum, AA/R Strange; **150** Rufino Tamayo Museum, AA/R Strange; **150/1** Oaxaca, AA/C Sawyer; **152/3** Oaxaca, AA; **153** Huatulco, AA/C Sawyer; **154** Mitla, AA/S Watkins; **155** Puerto Escondido, AA/C Sawyer; **156/7** Balloon seller, AA/C Sawyer; **158** Canon de Sumidero, AA/R Strange; **158/9** Musicians, AA/C Sawyer; **160** Villahermosa, AA/R Strange; **167** Fishing Boat, AA/R Strange; **168** Merida, AA/C Sawyer; **168/9t** Merida, AA/R Strange; **168/9b** Casa de Montejo, AA/C Sawyer; **170** Cathedral, AA/C Sawyer; **170/1** Campeche, AA/C Sawyer; **172** Cancun, AA/C Sawyer; **173** sun gleams off the Nohuch Mul Pyramid in Coba; **174** Coba, AA/R Strange; **175** Valladolid, AA/C Sawyer; **176/7t** Cozumel, AA/R Strange; **176/7b** Isla Mujeres, AA/C Sawyer; **178** Tulum, AA/P Wilson; **179** Playa del Carmen, AA/C Sawyer; **180** Uxmal, AA/R Strange.

Every effort has been made to trace the copyright holders, and we apologise in advance for any unintentional omissions or errors. We would be pleased to apply any corrections in a following edition of this publication.